The Inclusive Classroom

The Inclusive
Early Childhood Classroom

Easy Ways to Adapt
Learning Centers
for All Children

Patti Gould & Joyce Sullivan

Illustrations by Joan Waites

Photographs by Paul Baskett

Gryphon House
Lewisville, NC

Acknowledgments

With love and sincere thanks to
Our families, for their unwavering support.
Our colleagues, the teachers and therapists with whom we have collaborated and explored new ideas.
The parents and children we have worked with and from whom we have learned so much.

We have written this book as a guide for making modifications for the children in your classroom, but we recommend that you consult with an occupational or physical therapist as you implement our suggestions. (You may also contact us through our publisher's web site: www.gryphonhouse.com.)

Copyright © 1999 Patti Gould and Joyce Sullivan
www.inclusiveclassroom.com
Published by Gryphon House, Inc.
PO Box 10, Lewisville, NC 27023
800.638.0928 (toll free); 877.638.7576 (fax)

Visit us on the web at www.gryphonhouse.com

Printed in the United States of America.

Text Illustrations: Joan Waites

Photographs by Paul Baskett

Reprinted September 2018

Library of Congress Cataloging-in-Publication Data

Gould, Patti, 1949--
    The inclusive early childhood classroom : easy ways to adapt learning centers for all children / Patti Gould and Joyce Sullivan.
        p.   cm.
    Includes bibliographical references and index.
    ISBN 978-0-87659-203-8
    1. Inclusive education--United States. 2. Handicapped children--Education (Early Childhood)--United States. I. Sullivan, Joyce, 1952- . II. Title.
    LC1201.G68   1998
    371.9'046--dc21   99-26410
                                                              CIP

Gryphon House books are available at special discount when purchased in bulk or special premiums and sales promotions as well as for fund-raising use. Special editions or book excerpts also can be created to specification. For details, contact the Director of Marketing at PO Box 10, Lewisville, NC 27023.

"I'm a Little Teapot" written by Clarence Kelley and George Sanders. Copyright © 1939 Kelman Music Corporation. Copyright renewed 1967 by Marilyn Sanders O'Bradovich. International Copyright Secured. All rights reserved.

The Inclusive Classroom

Table of Contents

Preface

The inclusion model is now widely accepted as the best way to educate children with special needs. Inclusion brings young children with special needs into public and private schools, childcare centers, preschool programs, Head Start programs, and family childcare. Although some children with special needs can be easily absorbed into the existing framework without significant modifications, most children with special needs require at least some revision of teaching modalities, curriculum, environment, and personnel. Who decides which changes need to be made and how to implement them? Teachers, parents, and specialists work together to come up with a plan and then establish a system of ongoing communication that enables them to address new challenges as they arise.

Many teachers, however, are overwhelmed by the impact that inclusion has had on their ability to run a successful program. Childcare providers and preschool, kindergarten, and primary teachers often have had little training in working with children with special needs and are not familiar with how to integrate children with disabilities into the classroom. Therapists and specialists who work with these children serve as a resource for the teachers, but a typical work day does not offer enough time for the teachers and therapists to exchange information and explore solutions. Although therapists may be experts when it comes to working with children with special needs, they frequently lack experience in the curriculum planning and implementation that is necessary for a successful educational program. The well-meaning therapist may suggest activities to teachers that might help the child with special needs, but may not easily fit into the overall scheme of the classroom or accommodate the teacher's personal style. It is not uncommon for teachers to refer to these activity suggestions as just "one more thing to do" in an already harried schedule.

The Inclusive Early Childhood Classroom is not an activity book or a curriculum planning guide. Nor is it a collection of therapeutic interventions. Rather, our book is a resource manual on how to adapt "regular" curriculum activities for children with special needs. We offer concrete suggestions that are easy to implement and give teachers the tools to make their classrooms into effective learning environments for all students. Many of these modifications are useful and interesting to the other children in the classroom, so that no one child needs to feel different or inferior.

In writing this book we have struggled with the distinction between developmentally appropriate practice and teacher-directed approaches. The current thought in early childhood education is that all learning should be child-initiated. Many children with special needs, however, benefit from activities and interventions that are more structured and repetitive in nature and, therefore,

Table of Contents

need to be planned and implemented by an adult. We believe that both approaches to early childhood education are valid as long as the child's needs are being addressed. Our goal is to provide teachers, therapists, and parents with simple modifications to help **all** children stay engaged and involved in center activities. By staying focused on the activities, the materials, and the social interactions of the classroom, children with special needs have the opportunity to learn new skills and concepts along with their peers.

The Inclusive Early Childhood Classroom is arranged in teacher-friendly chapters: circle time, art center, sand and water center, block center, dramatic play, snack time, transitions, fine motor center, and gross motor center. Each chapter is divided into six disability categories that are based partly on medical diagnoses and partly on how each disability affects the child's ability to learn and function. For instance, children who are blind and children who are partially sighted are grouped together in a category we call children with visual impairments. Children who are disruptive and do not respond to commonly used behavior management techniques and children with a diagnosis of Attention Deficit/Hyperactivity Disorder are grouped together in a category called Attention Deficit/Hyperactivity Disorder (ADHD) and Behavioral Issues.

The six disability groupings we have chosen to use are (1) children with mental handicaps and developmental delays; (2) children with orthopedic impairments; (3) children with ADHD and behavioral issues; (4) children with Pervasive Developmental Disorder (PDD) or autism; (5) children with motor planning problems, and (6) children with visual impairments. We are aware that many children will not fit neatly into these particular categories and some children might display characteristics that overlap two or more disability groupings; however, we believe that our system of disability categories offers a clear and easy way to access the information we have compiled.

In chapter one there are checklists to help you figure out which disability grouping(s) best corresponds to a particular child in your classroom. These checklists are not meant to be used for diagnostic purposes but to guide you to the section of the book that might be most useful. For instance, after reading the checklists you might decide that a particular child in your classroom exhibits some of the characteristics described on the Attention Deficit/Hyperactivity Disorder (ADHD) and Behavioral Issues checklist. You are concerned about this child's overall functioning, but you note that one of the most difficult parts of the day for this child is transition time. Using these two pieces of information about the child, you would turn to the chapter on transition time and read over the suggestions in the section on children with Attention Deficit/Hyperactivity Disorder (ADHD) and Behavioral Issues. You might find one or two modifications that you can use immediately. Even though the other suggestions might not seem appropriate for this particular child, your particular classroom, or your style of teaching, you might still benefit by reading through the entire section in order to get a general sense of how to work with the child. In fact, we urge you to review all the modifications in the transition chapter because you might find a suggestion in another disability section that you want to try.

Our book also has an appendix that describes the general sensory needs of children, simple adaptations to make and use, and a list of commercially available materials.

We have written this book as a guide for making modifications for the children in your classroom, but we recommend that you consult with an occupational or physical therapist as you implement our suggestions. (You may contact us through our publisher's Web site: www.gryphonhouse.com.)

Overview

All children in early childhood classrooms need nurturing and stimulating learning environments, but for children with special needs, many typical experiences need to be modified to promote their development. These modifications can, at times, seem overwhelming to the busy classroom teacher who must consider whether to modify the environment, the classroom equipment and materials, the activities, or the expectations that they have of the child. In *The Inclusive Early Childhood Classroom* we suggest different ways of doing typical activities and routines so that children with special needs will be successful.

Each chapter of *The Inclusive Early Childhood Classroom* describes modifications to use in centers or typical classroom routines for children with various types of special needs. Although we understand that differences may exist among these children in terms of their behaviors and needs, we have grouped the modifications into six categories.

Developmental Delays

These children attain skill mastery at a slower rate than other children. Some may be delayed due to environmental factors and will eventually catch up if they are given appropriate instruction. Some children with developmental delays may have mental retardation. Children with mental retardation are more likely to have problems with hearing, vision, attention, and seizures. There are many levels of mental retardation, but all except the most severely impaired are able to learn new skills.

Orthopedic Impairments

This category might include children with cerebral palsy, spina bifida, muscular dystrophy, congenital anomalies, rheumatoid arthritis, fractures, or burns (Safford 1989). The child's ability to learn may or may not be affected. Cerebral palsy is a group of conditions characterized by motor problems that result from damage to the brain early in the developmental process. The child may have tightness and/or weakness on one side of the body, in the legs only, or throughout the body. Muscular dystrophy becomes obvious at about age three, with muscles weakening as the child becomes older. Spina bifida is a hereditary problem where the spine does not close properly, which can result in paralysis of the lower body. In osteogenisis imperfecta the bones break easily, and in juvenile rheumatoid arthritis there is chronic and painful inflammation of the joints.

Pervasive Developmental Disorder (PDD) and Autism

Pervasive developmental disorder is an umbrella term that includes autistic disorder, any pervasive developmental disorder not otherwise specified, and Asperger's syndrome. Recently these disorders have also been grouped under the heading of Autism Specturm Disorder. Typical children with pervasive developmental disorder or autism have delays in language and social skills that are present before thirty months of age. There may be an insistence on sameness as shown by limited play skills, an abnormal preoccupation with particular play routines (perseveration), and resisting change. The child may be oversensitive to certain kinds of sensory input from the environment. PDD/Autism is a spectrum disorder with some children being mildly involved and having average or above average intelligence and other children having more severe involvement with mental retardation.

Attention Deficit/Hyperactivity Disorder (ADHD) and Behavioral Issues

This category includes children with an array of behavioral issues due to either environmental or biological factors. Although most physicians do not diagnose Attention Deficit/Hyperactivity Disorder (ADHD) until the child is five or six years old, we see children in preschool and kindergarten who exhibit characteristics similar to those described by ADHD. Of course, many three- or four-year-olds are active and distractible, but the degree to which this behavior is manifested and interferes with skill acquisition is what separates a typical high activity level from one that is dysfunctional. These children are often in constant motion and may not have had adequate practice in basic developmental skills.

Motor Planning Problems

The child with motor planning problems has difficulty planning and carrying out unfamiliar movements. The problem seems to be the formulation of the plan, as well as coordinating the movements necessary to carry out the plan. The child may also have poor quality of movement; for example, he can catch a ball, but does so in a clumsy way with exaggerated movements. These children need accurate information from their senses to be successful in moving (Johnson-Martin, Attermeier, and Hacker 1990).

Visual Impairments

Up to sixty percent of children with visual impairments have other disabilities, including cerebral palsy, mental retardation, and hearing impairment. Visual impairments range from minor deficits in visual acuity, where corrective lenses fix most of the problem, to total blindness. Eye function varies with the time of day, lighting, and weather patterns. A child may be able to complete a task one day but not the next. Some children may appear to be turning away from the activity, but they are using their peripheral vision. Children with visual impairments frequently exhibit sensory defensiveness, especially to touching textures such as clay, sand, goop, and fingerpaint.

The modifications in each chapter will help all children stay involved in developmentally appropriate routines and center-based activities, enabling them to learn. The more time the child is engaged, the more the child learns (McCormick, Noonan, and Heck 1997). Keeping track of what a child learns is essential; therefore, it is important to identify goals that are relevant to the child's developmental needs and to keep data on how the child is progressing. The following forms were designed to make it easier to organize learning programs for children. While all the forms are based on our years of experience, we suggest that you modify the forms to suit your children's needs. There are three kinds of forms. The first kind (pages16–21) are helpful in targeting skills a particular child needs to learn in the classroom. These forms can be used when writing the child's educational plan and to generate information to include in performance and instructional profiles. The second kind of form (pages 22–31) details modifications for daily activities (such as circle time, snack, and transitions), and the following centers: art, sand and water, blocks, dramatic play, fine motor, and gross motor. These forms can be posted on clipboards in the classroom or centers. The third type of form (page 32) targets skills children are developing. The teacher identifies and records a skill for each of the classroom centers, or focuses on one or two centers. The teacher may want to keep one of these forms for each of the children, to collect data on the child's progress.

The forms in this chapter outline the information that is presented in more depth in the rest of the book. Refer to these chapters if you are unclear on any of the modifications listed. We have tried to include modifications that would be easy for teachers to do so that all children can participate successfully. Use only those modifications that will increase the skills and independence of the children in your classroom.

Teachers in integrated classrooms function as part of a team with physical, occupational, and speech therapists. Parents are also an important part of this team. Children achieve the greatest success when modifications and adaptations are developed by the team. You may need to speak to a therapist about individualizing a technique, position, or adaptation that has been described in this book. Set aside time to get together and establish goals, and, later on, to review the child's progress. We hope that these forms simplify the process. Each form has a space for teachers to list additional modifications that they have discovered. Teaching assistants, substitute teachers, or volunteers may also find these forms helpful when working with children in the classroom.

Developmental Delays

Child's name _____ Date of birth _____

Diagnosis _____

Check any of the following that apply
___ has difficulty learning new skills
___ exhibits low muscle tone
___ demonstrates disruptions in eating and/or sleeping patterns
___ stays with an activity for only a minute or two
___ is easily distracted by noise and visual stimuli
___ appears lethargic
___ body is in constant motion
___ has difficulty understanding verbal directions
___ likes to touch and hug other children
___ exhibits delays in fine motor skills
___ exhibits delays in gross motor skills
___ exhibits delays in language skills
___ exhibits delays in social skills
___ needs assistance with dressing
___ needs assistance with feeding
___ needs assistance with toileting
___ bumps into things and falls down frequently

Check any of the following strategies that will help the child with developmental delays in your classroom
___ Simplify tasks by reducing the number of steps, using backward chaining and plenty of modeling and cues.
___ Incorporate structure and routine into the child's day. Routines allow the child to anticipate events and provide multiple opportunities to repeat and practice skills.
___ Remember that while most skills will develop in the expected developmental sequence, occasionally a child will skip a few levels to master a higher level skill. If a child does this, do not assume that now the child is also able to perform all the in-between skills.
___ Simplify the language that you use with the child. Short phrases repeated in a rhythmic cadence or sung to a familiar tune can be effective for communicating directions.
___ Encourage activities that will develop the child's body concept such as large movement games that include rolling, crawling, walking backwards and sideways, jumping, and other movement variations.
___ Use bookcases, table top carrels, or other types of dividers to reduce visual distractions when trying to work on specific skills.
___ Provide many opportunities for the child to practice and repeat the skills that he is working on.
___ Maintain eye contact with the child when speaking. Cue the child to maintain eye contact with the activity that he is engaged in.
___ Shorten activities to correspond to the child's attention span.
___ Provide adapted utensils, tools, or fasteners as needed to encourage independence.

Describe additional modifications _____
_____

Checklist

Child's name _____ Date of birth _____

Diagnosis_____

Check any of the following that apply

___ has a difficult time remaining upright

___ poor head control

___ deformities that limit the child's ability to function

___ tires easily

___ abnormal reflexes

___ abnormal muscle tone on just one side ___ right ___ left

___ abnormal muscle tone in the legs only

___ abnormal muscle tone throughout the body

___ low muscle tone/appears floppy

___ high muscle tone/appears stiff

___ problems with coordination and balance

___ difficulty keeping lips closed, drooling

___ tremors

___ seizures

___ unable to walk without help

___ unable to sit without help

___ joint pain

___ bones break easily

___ difficulty swallowing

___ does not use verbal language

Check any of the following strategies that will help the child with orthopedic impairments in your classroom

___ Position the child carefully so that he is sitting with his hips bent and head and back in alignment.

___ Make sure that tables and chairs are helping the child to stay upright.

___ Stabilize learning materials with suction cups, clamps, or Velcro.

___ Provide alternative methods of communication such as picture icons.

___ Provide electric switches to activate toys.

___ Make items easier to grasp by adding foam tubing.

___ Position items on table top easels to help maintain an upright position.

___ The child may need a chair with sides.

___ Watch for signs of fatigue; it is counterproductive for children to exhaust themselves.

___ Encourage the child to use two hands in activities.

___ If the child has tight muscles, avoid resistive activities such as playing with stiff playdough.

___ Warn the child before picking him up or moving him.

___ Make sure furniture in the room can support the weight of a child pulling to stand.

___ Change the child's position frequently unless medically contraindicated.

Describe additional modifications _____

_____

checklist

Pervasive Developmental Disorder (PDD) and Autism

Child's name _____ Date of birth_____

Diagnosis _____

Check any of the following that apply

_____ disruption in language

_____ disruption in social skills

_____ insistence on sameness, stereotyped play, resistance to change

_____ overreacts to some kinds of sensory input (example: panics over sight of rubber gloves)

_____ may seem to ignore other kinds of sensory input (example: completely ignores his teacher)

_____ self-stimulation noted

_____ difficulty making eye contact

_____ difficulty attending to activities not of his choosing

_____ resistance to adult-directed tasks

_____ echolalic speech—child repeats what is said to him

_____ lack of imaginary play

Check any of the following modifications that will help the child with pervasive developmental disorder or autism in your classroom

_____ Use direct instruction to teach the following task _____.

_____ Teach peer partners to approach the child.

_____ Observe what peers are doing in a center and teach the child with autism to do the same thing or participate in some meaningful way.

_____ Use a variety of reinforcers.

_____ Use picture icons and/or sign language to make directions clear.

_____ Use short, concise statements.

_____ Respond sensitively to the child's ability (or inability) to handle environmental stimuli.

_____ Initially use one-to-one instruction and gradually add more group work.

_____ Model language using the pronoun "I." Instead of saying, "Tommy is going up the slide," say, "I am going up the slide." The child who is echolalic will repeat the phrase using the correct pronoun and eventually incorporate the use of "I" into his speech.

_____ Observe what is going on when the child is focused and interactive during activities. If he enjoys having a certain child nearby or really likes to play in certain activities, use that information to help him to be successful in other activities.

_____ Schedule sensory experiences that are calming into the child's day. For example, if the child finds slow back-and-forth swinging to be calming, plan to regularly swing the child for five to ten minutes before work time. Notice if the swinging is actually calming the child and stop if it is not.

_____ When the child needs to work on a skill or try an experience, insist on the child's participation. If the child feels he can get out of the experience by crying or resisting, he will use this more and more to escape adult-directed tasks. Always use positive reinforcers when the child cooperates.

_____ Create a sensory diet for the child that will help the child to modulate his responses to environmental stimulation. If the child seems overstimulated, provide more relaxing input such as taking slow deep breaths, or lying on large pillows. Try dimming the lights in the classroom. Use a soft calm voice if the child seems overstimulated. Some children find deep pressure calming.

_____ Try weighted vests, lying under a mattress or gym mat, rolling up in a blanket, or wearing a T-shirt that is one size too small.

_____ Allow the child to stand for some activities; sitting for long periods can be difficult.

Describe additional modifications _____

_____

checklist

Attention Deficit/Hyperactivity Disorder (ADHD) and Behavioral Issues

Child's name _____ Date of birth_____

Diagnosis _____

Check any of the following that apply

____ cannot attend to any activity for more than a couple of minutes

____ body is in constant motion

____ acts impulsively and does not consider the consequences

____ is easily distracted by sounds

____ is easily distracted by visual stimuli

____ has difficulty following simple directions

____ frequently gets into fights with other children

____ difficulty remaining seated during circle time

____ likes to participate in rough and tumble play

____ crashes into walls, floors, or soft furniture

____ becomes easily frustrated by new tasks

____ invades other children's personal space

____ exhibits delays in fine motor skills

____ exhibits delays in language skills

____ exhibits delays in cognitive skills

____ needs assistance with self-help skills

Check any of the following strategies that will help the child with ADHD and behavioral issues in your classroom

____ Help the child calm and organize his nervous system by providing opportunities for proprioceptive input. Examples include heavy work such as carrying the large wooden blocks or scrubbing tabletops, wearing a backpack filled with books, or wearing a weighted vest.

____ Provide proprioceptive input to the mouth: chewing on flexible rubber tubing or on resistive food snacks such as bagels. For additional information on sensory processing problems see the appendix.

____ Provide quiet spaces where the child can go when he needs a break from the distractions of the classroom. Three examples are (1) place a large empty appliance carton in a corner of the room, cut a door in one side, and pad the inside with some cushions; (2) set up a small tent—some toy stores sell child-size tents that do not take up much space; and (3) throw a blanket, tablecloth, or sheet over a small table and put a few pillows under the table.

____ Try to reduce the amount of noise in the room by using carpeting or hanging a drop ceiling.

____ Minimize visual distractions by using a table-top divider or carrels to define private spaces.

____ Play soft instrumental music to calm the child; music with words generally is not calming.

____ Note if the child has more difficulty during one part of day. Try to restructure the day. Maybe the child would do better if circle time were scheduled earlier or later in the day.

____ Allow children to wear a jacket or sweater if they are sensitive to touch . Covering the bare skin minimizes the physical contact the child might have with other children who unintentionally touch the child.

____ There are many successful systems of behavior management. Adopt the one that not only addresses the needs of the child, but also is consistent with your school's philosophy, fits your particular style of teaching, and is consistent with the family's style of behavior management.

____ For children with behavioral concerns, it is always important that the activity match the developmental level of the child. Because it is already difficult for the child to attend to task, imagine how much more difficult it is when the activity is too hard.

____ Plan the day so quiet activities alternate with more active movement experiences.

Describe additional modifications _____

_____

Checklist

Motor Planning Problems

Child's name _____ Date of birth_____

Diagnosis _____

Check any of the following that apply
____ difficulty planning and executing unfamiliar movements
____ poor quality of movement (for example, the child can catch a ball, but does so with poor coordination)
____ low tolerance for frustration
____ fearful of trying new activities
____ bumps into things in the classroom
____ does not use tools efficiently
____ has difficulty knowing where he has been touched
____ difficulty building with manipulatives
____ difficulty sticking with tasks

Check any of the following strategies that will help the child with motor planning problems in your classroom
____ Start with larger objects and move to smaller ones.
____ Weighted objects may be easier to handle.
____ When teaching a new skill, present a "just right" challenge by carefully breaking the activity into small sequential steps.
____ Use play themes or toys that are of high interest to the child when presenting more challenging activities.
____ Having the child wear a weighted vest or play with heavy toys such as wooden blocks may give him a better sense of himself in space. Leave the vest on for only 10-15 minutes at a time.
____ Allow the child to play on the floor, lying on his tummy and supported on his forearms to strengthen his shoulders.
____ The child might be better off sitting in a chair at circle time rather than on the floor if he is having difficulty maintaining a seated position.
____ Teach shortcuts for classroom routines. Rather than carrying one toy at a time during cleanup, provide the child with a small basket to collect several toys to put away. This may lessen the chances the child will be tripping over toys and other children.
____ Children with motor planning problems benefit from simple gross motor experiences such as learning to climb up and slide down a small slide. Give the child lots of verbal and physical cues to help him through the activity.
____ Encourage the child to tell you how he plans to approach an unfamiliar task.
____ Help the child to generalize learned skills to new activities. For example, if the child has learned to jump on a small trampoline, explain that the same kind of jumping can be used to hop in and out of hudqla hoops. Provide opportunities to practice jumping in a variety of activities (Fisher, Murray, and Bundy 1991).
____ Give the child time to observe other children before joining in movement activities.
____ Sometimes the child may just need help starting an activity, but will be able to finish it independently.

Describe additional modifications _____
_____

Checklist

Child's name_____ Date of birth_____

Diagnosis _____

Check any of the following that apply

____ wears corrective lenses

____ holds objects close to face

____ always seems to turn head to side; uses peripheral vision

____ bends head down close to table surface

____ rubs eyes frequently

____ exhibits mannerisms such as arm flapping, rocking, eye poking, or light gazing

____ avoids bright lights

____ does not like to touch textures such as clay, sand, goop, fingerpaint

____ has also been diagnosed with cerebral palsy

____ has also been diagnosed with a hearing impairment

____ has also been diagnosed with mental retardation

____ is hesitant about participating in activities

____ prefers to stay in one play center

____ unable to find way about the room

____ needs assistance with dressing, toileting, and/or feeding

____ holds head down while talking to others

____ startles easily

____ frequently falls

Check any of the following strategies that will help the child with visual impairments in your classroom

____ Encourage the child to use whatever vision he has.

____ Adjust lighting by either making the room brighter or dimmer, according to the child's needs.

____ Mark areas of the room with easily identifiable tactile objects.

____ Reduce glare. Use shades on windows but have good, even overhead lighting. Use a dull finish on tabletop surfaces and matte (flat) paint for walls.

____ Keep noise level in room down and reduce extraneous visual stimuli.

____ Watch for signs of fatigue: yawning, eye rubbing, blinking, eye rolling, distant gaze.

____ Work with parents, counselor, psychologist, or vision specialist to set up consistent cues to help reduce inappropriate mannerisms common to blind children (hand waving, flicking fingers in front of eyes, rocking, arm flapping, light gazing, eye poking, eye rubbing).

____ Use consistent labels for objects. For instance, don't say "cat" one day and "kitty" the next. Teach the child consistent routines in the classroom to encourage independence.

____ Keep the child constructively involved in activities in order to discourage a pattern of repetitive self-stimulatory behaviors (Clark and Allen 1985).

____ Encourage gradual exploration of different textures and surfaces.

____ Warn the child before touching him.

____ Walk in front or next to the child, not behind.

____ Speak to the child using a normal volume and tone of voice.

____ Actively assist the child to explore his environment. If the child has bumped into or tripped over something, help the child to go back and explore the obstacle visually or by touch. Investigate the source of loud noises or any other stimuli that frighten the child. Use bright fluorescent colors like red, yellow, pink, and orange in activities or to modify toys to encourage use of vision.

Describe additional modifications _____

_____

Checklist

Circle Time

Check any of the following strategies you plan to use during circle time
____ Shorten circle time to match the attention span of the children in your classroom.
____ Divide children into smaller circle time groupings.
____ Schedule circle time during a different part of the day.
____ Eliminate circle time completely.
____ Let children sit in chairs for circle time.
____ Allow children to hold a stuffed animal or fidget toy.
____ Seat children so that there is at least one foot of space between them.
____ Remind children frequently of circle time rules.
____ Make circle time optional, just like the other play centers.
____ Incorporate movement and/or music into most circle time activities.
____ Have a circle time routine; for example, present the same activities in the same order.
____ Let the children munch on a snack during circle time.
____ Assign circle time jobs to all the children.
____ Have alternative seating available such as a beanbag chair or a deep soft cushion.
____ Have a weighted backpack or vest available for the child to wear. Remove after 10-15 minutes.

Materials for circle time
____ carpet squares
____ hula hoops
____ masking tape
____ fidget toys
____ stuffed animals
____ musical instruments
____ puppets
____ snack
____ tape recorder
____ magnetic or Velcro-backed tags
____ rocking chair
____ beanbag chair
____ picture and icon cards
____ weighted vests
____ corner seat
____ big books
____ props for stories

Describe additional modifications _____
_____

Checklist

Art Center

Check any of the following strategies you plan to use in this center
____ Build up handles of paintbrushes, crayons, and markers.
____ Place each child's art project inside a shirt box or on a cookie sheet.
____ Provide a variety of sizes of coloring implements.
____ Use large paper surfaces taped to the wall or an easel at eye level.
____ Add thickeners, textures, and fragrances to paints.
____ Allow children to stand, kneel on a chair, or straddle a chair while playing at the art table.
____ Have stencils of simple geometric shapes available for children to use.
____ Try alternatives to white glue, such as tape, sticky paper, glue stick. Place pieces of precut tape along the edge of a weighted container.
____ Place only one or two collage materials out on the table at one time.
____ Make a tabletop easel out of a cardboard box.
____ Use high-contrast materials.
____ Use pastel paper instead of white.
____ Place paper on top of mesh screening or sandpaper.
____ Use study carrels to separate work spaces.
____ Prepare the child's hands with a warm-up clapping activity.
____ Experience cutting a variety of materials, not just paper.
____ Tape one end of the paper to the wall for cutting.
____ Hold the paper for the child while he is learning to cut.
____ Use a variety of scissors, including small scissors, designed for preschoolers (available through catalogs).
____ Use glue to outline forms for coloring or cutting.

Materials for the art center
____ cornstarch
____ screening
____ contact paper
____ standing easel
____ stencils
____ large sheets of paper
____ old greeting cards
____ food coloring
____ collage materials
____ white glue
____ glue sticks
____ paste
____ fingerpaints
____ chalk
____ markers, crayons, and paintbrushes of various lengths and diameters

____ sandpaper
____ double-sided tape
____ tabletop easel
____ cookie sheets
____ variety of scissors
____ wallpaper
____ straws

Describe additional modifications _____
_____

Checklist

Sand and Water Center

Check any of the following strategies you plan to use in this center

____ Limit the number of children at the sand and water table to two if the children who are present are easily overstimulated.

____ Adjust the height of the water table to the child's needs.

____ Remove wheels or stabilize table against a wall so that the table is not sliding around.

____ Break down directions into small steps.

____ Model language concepts such as big/small or full/empty.

____ Use sand and water play as an opportunity to get the child out of his wheelchair and onto his tummy to play on a wedge or in a prone stander. Speak to the child's therapist about positioning.

____ Make sure that there is adequate lighting over the sand and water table if the child has visual impairments.

____ Replace sand with heavier materials, such as pebbles, if the sand is too overstimulating.

____ Put sand in basins to define the child's play space.

____ Give clear and concise directions to help the child to expand play skills.

____ Provide enough play toys to lessen conflicts between children.

____ Use brightly colored toys that contrast with the sand.

____ Change water in the water table daily.

____ Supplement verbal directions with pictures or signs.

____ Introduce novel toys if the child's attention begins to fade.

____ Encourage sharing and interaction with other children.

____ If the child is anxious about water play, give the child time to observe other children and gradually have the child approach the water table.

Materials for the sand and water center

____ eyedroppers	____ basters	____ tongs
____ water pumps	____ sand shovels	____ sifters
____ scoops	____ coffee measures	____ spoons
____ squirt bottle	____ food coloring	____ shape molds
____ cookie cutters	____ water wheels	____ spoons
____ cups and containers	____ screw-on caps	____ sponges
____ basins	____ funnels	____ corks
____ scrub brushes	____ popsicle sticks	____ egg beaters
____ wooden beads	____ wooden blocks	____ tubing
____ bubble blowers	____ plastic people	____ plastic animals
____ trucks	____ plates and utensils	
____ spray bottles	____ egg cartons	
____ film canisters	____ ice cube trays	
____ toys that have contrasting colors		
____ adjustable sand/water table		

Describe additional modifications_____

_____

checklist

Block Center

Check any of the following strategies you plan to use in this center

____ Place a basket of blocks next to each child or pair of children.

____ Encourage children to use props such as toy animals and people, cars, and road signs.

____ Let each child use only a small number of blocks.

____ Use mats, tape, or other suitable material to define children's spaces.

____ Let the child lie on a wedge mat while building with blocks on the floor.

____ Encourage the child to build against a stable surface such as a wall.

____ Place carpeting in the block center to help reduce noise.

____ Remind children of block center rules frequently.

____ Rotate the types of blocks: plastic blocks, unit blocks, large wooden blocks, and cardboard blocks.

____ Use interlocking blocks such as Bristle Blocks or Duplos.

____ Encourage block activities that are at the child's developmental level. Filling up a container or dumping them out are legitimate block center activities.

____ Model imaginative play and provide opportunities for children to imitate your block structures and play.

____ Encourage children to build horizontally rather than vertically.

____ Allow children to build inside a large empty appliance box.

Materials for the block center

____ unit blocks

____ large wooden blocks

____ plastic blocks

____ cardboard blocks

____ Bristle Blocks

____ Duplos

____ preschool Legos

____ animal figures

____ human figures

____ cars, trucks

____ road signs

____ paper and tape

____ markers

____ toy furniture

____ pipe cleaners

____ small pieces of cloth

____ baskets

____ sections of indoor-outdoor carpeting

____ small cardboard or plastic boxes or containers

____ short pieces of string or shoelaces

Describe additional modifications _____

_____

Checklist

Dramatic Play Center

Check any of the following strategies you plan to use in this center

____ Let the child choose play that is of interest to him.

____ Provide direct instruction of play skills when needed.

____ Teach peer role models to include the child with special needs in play.

____ Set up boundaries to keep the children close to each other to encourage interaction.

____ Position children so that they can move to the best of their abilities.

____ Establish only those rules that are needed for the children to play safely.

____ Allow some roughhousing to provide children with an opportunity to learn to read the nonverbal cues of the other children.

____ Encourage children to verbalize their plans for play and to review what they did when the play is over.

____ Help parents to encourage dramatic play at home.

____ Create storybooks about the children's play and read frequently as a tool to teach play skills.

____ Dress-ups should be easy to get on and off.

____ Provide picture icons to help the child learn new play skills.

____ Teach children to use language to express feelings and resolve conflicts.

____ Partition off the dramatic play center by hanging sheets from the ceiling.

____ Assess the child's play skills by observing how he plays.

____ Avoid interrupting the child's play unless the child needs help to expand play.

____ While children are playing, stay involved by observing or playing with the children; don't use this as a time to talk to other adults.

____ If the children in your classroom tend to get overstimulated, play music with a slow, even beat while the children are in the dramatic play center.

Materials for the dramatic play center

____ cause-and-effect toys such as jack-in-the-box		____ construction toys
____ doctor kits	____ small plastic animals	
____ dolls	____ strollers	____ shopping carts
____ mirrors	____ picnic basket	____ kitchen equipment
____ toy plates and utensils	____ plastic food	____ cushions
____ telephones	____ tent	____ cash register
____ dress-ups with easy fasteners	____ stuffed animals	
____ boxes	____ battery-operated toys with switches	
____ briefcases	____ corner seats	
____ wedges	____ picture icons	
____ doll houses	____ water table for baby baths	
____ props for birthday party		
____ props for restaurant play (menu, aprons, plastic hamburger, plastic pizza)		
____ playdough		

Describe additional modifications _____

_____

Checklist

Snack Time

Check any of the following strategies you plan to use for snack time

____ Sit at the snack table to encourage interactions between children.

____ Let children set up and clean up their own snack.

____ Keep language the same from day to day when teaching snack routines to children with language impairments.

____ Use picture icons to cue children during snack.

____ Include toothbrushing as part of snack time.

____ Use vinyl rather than latex gloves to avoid allergic reactions.

____ Offer a variety of foods during snack.

____ Discuss eating problems with parents.

____ Use simple cooking activities to encourage functional fine motor skills.

____ Break eating skills into small sequential steps.

____ Contact the child's doctor or nutritionist if the child has special eating issues.

____ Set child in an appropriate size chair so that feet rest on the floor.

____ Have adaptive plates, cups, and utensils available.

____ Establish a small snack group if eating with the whole group at one time distracts the child.

____ Play calming music during snack.

____ Don't change too many variables at once when introducing new foods. For example, add graham crackers to a preferred food like pudding.

____ To avoid choking, give small amounts of food at one time to children who tend to eat too quickly.

____ Familiarize yourself with medications the child is taking and their side effects, especially the impact on appetite.

____ For the child who has facial muscle weakness, encourage bubble or whistle blowing. If the child is able to drink from a straw, provide thickened liquids to strengthen muscles in the face.

Materials for snack

____ vinyl gloves   ____ toothbrushes
____ cooking equipment   ____ Dycem, a rubberized non-slip material
____ utensils with built-up handles   ____ weighted utensils
____ swivel utensils   ____ straws
____ bent utensils   ____ cup with cutout for a child's nose
____ cups with two handles   ____ cuff with pocket for utensils
____ blender   ____ table top mirror
____ nuk massager   ____ placemats
____ trays

Describe additional modifications _____

_____

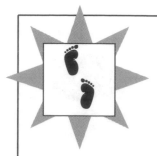

Transitions

Check any of the following strategies you plan to use during transition times

____ Build routines into arrival and departure times.

____ Maintain consistent routines from day to day.

____ Use adaptive dressing/undressing techniques that promote independence.

____ Post a pictorial representation of the day's schedule.

____ Use arrival time as an opportunity to do large movement and active play.

____ Plan transitions from one activity to the next in small groups rather than as one large group.

____ Use waiting time constructively; practice a song or fingerplay, imitate facial expressions.

____ Let the child take a transition toy from one center into the next.

____ Provide reminders that an activity is about to end.

____ Have children return to the rug area between activities.

____ Rearrange furniture to provide clear traffic paths.

____ Use backward chaining to teach dressing skills.

____ Encourage parents to dress children in clothing that is easy for children to get on and off.

____ Have the same adult greet the children each morning.

____ Make coat hooks and cubbies accessible to wheelchair-bound children.

____ Use transition cards or tickets that have a picture of the next activity.

____ Offer children frequent choices to change centers/activities.

____ Incorporate transition songs, clean-up time songs, hello and good-bye songs.

Materials for transitions

____ picture or icon cards

____ modified clothing using Velcro, larger button holes, or shower curtain ring

____ long rope

____ schedule of the day in pictures

____ dressing cue cards

____ painted lines, Velcro strips, or varied floor covering for clear boundary indicators

____ activity cue cards

____ center tags

Describe additional modifications _____

_____

Checklist

Fine Motor Center

Check any of the following strategies you plan to use in this center

____ Self-help skills are great for working on fine motor strength and dexterity. Encourage children to attempt buttons, zippers, and snaps, giving them only as much assistance as they need.

____ Encourage parents to involve children in household chores such as ripping up junk mail, folding facecloths, or picking up toys.

____ Make sure activities are of interest to the child to capture the child's attention. Include some of the following tasks in your fine motor centers:

∞ snipping paper of various thicknesses

∞ snaps, buttons, and zippers

∞ pushing small items through slits made in the plastic lids of containers

∞ dressing and undressing dolls, washing doll clothes and hanging them on a line to dry

∞ woodworking, hammering, sanding

∞ planting seeds.

____ Provide plenty of small manipulatives to encourage hand dexterity.

____ Many children need a non-distracting setting when learning new fine motor skills. Block distractions with partitions by hanging fabric from the ceiling, using bookcases, or purchasing commercial table top dividers.

____ Define children's play spaces with individual cookie sheets, shirt boxes, or placemats.

____ Provide a non-slip surface by placing rubbery shelving material or a piece of rug mat on the table.

____ Divide manipulatives into small, clear containers or shallow pans to reduce clutter.

____ Use manipulatives on the floor as well as on a table top.

____ Encourage children to talk about what they are doing while they are playing with manipulatives.

____ Stabilize the base of a fine motor activity by taping or clamping it to the table.

____ Try a variety of manipulative sizes to find the best "fit" for the child.

____ Some manipulatives can be positioned at a vertical surface by propping them on an easel or taping them to the wall.

____ Use heavy manipulatives, such as tuna fish cans, to stack.

Materials for the fine motor center

____ geoboards

____ hammering sets

____ pop beads and other interlocking toys

____ Bristle Blocks

____ shape boxes

____ wooden blocks of various sizes

____ Legos

____ Tinkertoys

____ snap blocks

____ Duplos

____ wooden beads and strings

____ lacing

____ stringing to make necklaces

____ eyedroppers

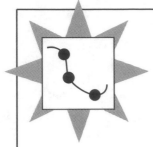

____ string hair rollers

____ buttons

____ straws

____ thread spools

____ toilet paper rolls

____ paper clips

____ puzzles

____ nesting cups

____ pegs and peg boards

____ games such as Mr. Potato Head, Lite Brite, or Bedbugs

____ tops

____ wind-up toys

____ clothespins

____ rolling pin

____ tweezers

____ tongs

____ tape

____ golf tees

____ clay

____ playdough

____ button boards

____ garlic press

____ plastic knives

Describe additional modifications _____

_____

Checklist

Gross Motor Center

Check any of the following strategies you plan to use in this center
____ Include gross motor activities as part of the curriculum each day.
____ Give children opportunities to plan and problem solve in gross motor activities.
____ Whenever possible, schedule gross motor activities to take place outside.
____ Follow large muscle activities with quiet activities.
____ Teachers should approach large muscle activities with enthusiasm.
____ Praise/reinforce the child's attempts at gross motor activities.
____ Encourage children to wear sneakers.
____ Convince parents of the importance of an active lifestyle at home.
____ Use exercise videos as a way of establishing an exercise routine.
____ Design gross motor activities at the child's current level of skill.
____ Work with therapists to provide functional movement experiences for the child
      with orthopedic involvement.
____ Use pictures when explaining movement experiences.
____ Start with one step directions.
____ Use hula hoops or rug squares to define personal space during movement experi-
      ences.
____ Heavy work, such as moving heavy wooden blocks, may help to calm children.
____ Encourage the child to verbalize his plan for attempting a gross motor activity.
____ Let the child with visual impairments explore unfamiliar gross motor equipment visu-
      ally and/or through touch before participating.
____ If the child is always using one kind of gross motor equipment, encourage involve-
      ment in less familiar activities.
____ Provide adaptive playground equipment.
____ Encourage interaction between children in the sand box.
____ Invite peer role models to demonstrate activities.

Equipment for the gross motor center

____ scooter boards	____ wagons
____ ball on string	____ rocking horse
____ cloth catchers mitt and ball with Velcro strips	____ tunnels
____ hula hoops	____ hippity hop ball
____ indoor and outdoor climbing structures	____ various kinds of swings
____ rope	____ ball pit
____ slides	____ music tapes
____ sand box	____ balls of various sizes
____ beanbags	____ Koosh balls
____ tricycles	____ wheeled equipment
____ prone standers	____ mats
____ weighted vests	____ exercise videos
____ small portable basketball hoops	____ roller skates
____ wheelbarrows	____ play lawn mowers
____ bowling games	____ foam mats
____ bubble solution and wands	____ crepe paper streamers
____ parachute	____ large cardboard boxes
____ balance beams	

Describe additional modifications _____

_____

31

Checklist

skill Development

Child's name_____Date of birth _____
Date _____

Time of Day or Center	Skill	Code
Arrival and Departure	_____	_____
Circle Time	_____	_____
Art Center	_____	_____
Block Center	_____	_____
Sand and Water Table	_____	_____
Dramatic Play	_____	_____
Snack Time	_____	_____
Transitions	_____	_____
Fine Motor Center	_____	_____
Gross Motor Center	_____	_____

Code:
A = achieved
P = more practice is needed
E = skill is emerging

checklist

Circle Time

Circle time is when the children come together to share the news of the day, read a story, sing, play rhythm instruments, assign jobs, or play a game. Some circle times also incorporate an attendance activity, such as placing attendance tags on a board or counting the number of girls and boys present. Circle time can introduce children to group listening and turn-taking skills, promote the development of language and social skills, and provide children with information about how their day will be structured.

Most three-year-olds and many four-year-olds are not developmentally ready to sit and listen to a group activity for longer than just a few minutes. Even with older children, it's a good idea to start the year with a short circle time that lasts three to five minutes and gradually lengthen it when the children are ready. Circle time activities that incorporate music and movement usually hold children's attention for longer periods of time than a sit-and-listen type of activity. You might want to begin the year with simple movement and music circle times and gradually develop a routine that balances active movement with quiet listening activities.

Although the traditional circle time includes all the children in the classroom, you might want to consider other options. For instance, make circle time an activity center and, like other play centers, give children the option of joining. Or run two circle times of eight children each instead of one large circle time of sixteen. Another option is to eliminate circle time completely until you feel the class is ready for this type of large group experience.

Common themes run through the ideas and suggestions for the disability groupings in this chapter. One of them, the most important, is the need to provide the consistency and structure that many children with special needs must have to thrive. Most young children need some degree of consistency and structure, but children with behavioral issues, PDD, autism, developmental delays, motor planning problems, and visual impairments need it even more. Providing these children with a regular circle time routine allows them to feel comfortable and in control of the world around them. Routine means that you do the same activities in the same order every day. As you repeat the same activity for a period of weeks, the children are able to practice and eventually master the skills necessary for that particular activity. These skills might include learning the words to a song, understanding a story, or simply passing a ball around the circle. For those of you who like to be creative with circle times, we advise you to introduce changes slowly while still maintaining the original framework. For instance, you might keep the opening and closing activities of circle time the same, but change some aspect of the middle activity. Sameness and routine is calming for many children, even though it might seem boring to you.

The importance of demonstrating new activities is another common theme. This is beneficial for both children with special needs and typically developing children. It is important to break down a new activity into its component steps and provide extra cues for each step. Extra cues might mean telling the child what you are doing as you demonstrate the activity. You can also add visual cues such as placing a paper bracelet on each child's right hand for a game of using one hand to pass a ball around a circle or drawing a chalk line on the floor for walking heel to toe. Touch cues might include a light tap to a particular body part or rubbing the arms and legs to wake them up before the activity. Incorporating as many of the senses as you can, especially when teaching a new circle time activity, is beneficial for all children.

A common theme in the circle time suggestions is allowing children to use fidget toys. Many adults have their own socially acceptable fidget accommodations that include doodling on a pad of paper, twirling a pen, playing with a paper clip, or picking at our nails. The physical act of manipulating an object in our hands helps us focus and can do the same for young children. Keep a basket of circle time fidget buddies near your circle time area. These toys might include small stuffed animals, plastic twisty snakes, and small rubber squeeze toys (the kind that do not whistle). Allow each child to choose one circle time buddy as a special friend for circle time. If choosing circle time buddies becomes problematic because two children want the same toy, consider assigning circle time buddies to each child.

Another common theme is providing a circle time space for each child. Many teachers already use small mats or carpet squares for seated circle time activities to provide structure to the circle and maintain physical distance between the children. We suggest that you use this idea for movement activities. Individual areas for movement games help some children who lack self-control, such as those with developmental delays, ADHD, and behavioral issues. A designated movement space for each child also creates a safety zone for a child who might be fearful of movement or afraid of bumping into others such as children with motor planning problems, PDD, autism, and visual impairments. With large hoops or masking tape squares on the rug, you can make each child's space large enough to accommodate movements on hands and knees, running in place, and jumping.

Following are specific suggestions for each of the special needs categories. Try them just as they are or modify them to meet the needs of the particular children in your group. Remember that you, the teacher, are the ultimate judge of which suggestions will work for the children in your classroom.

Developmental Delays

The child with developmental delays may "misbehave" during circle time. This behavior might be due to the child's inability to understand a complex language-based activity that is above her cognitive level, or it might be that the child is simply not developmentally ready to sit still for that length of time. Carefully consider the developmental level of the child to determine whether she should be expected to sit for a few minutes of circle time or be allowed to play quietly in another center. On the other hand, some children with developmental delays thrive on the circle time experience because it is a non–threatening, teacher-controlled opportunity to practice social skills. Weigh the strengths and weaknesses of each child to determine the best way to include her in circle time.

▲ Allow the developmentally delayed child to hold a "fidget" toy to keep her visually occupied, especially if the circle activity is language based with little movement. Fidget toys might include squishy balls, twisty snakes, lacing cards, or pliable animal figures. See page 187 in the appendix for more suggestions on fidget toys.

▲ Do not expect the child to stay at circle time for longer than two to three minutes. Start circle time with an activity that is developmentally appropriate for this child so she will be able to be successful. Once higher level activities are introduced, the developmentally delayed child might lose interest and need to be directed to another center to play quietly alone, with an assistant teacher or aide, or with one other child.

▲ Incorporate music, movement, props, and puppetry into circle time activities that might not otherwise hold the child's attention. For instance, sing the names of the days of the week, have a puppet talk about the weather, and count the boys and girls in the class by placing a green crown on each boy's head and a red crown on each girl's. Even though some of the concepts might be above the child's cognitive level, the developmentally delayed child will still gain language and social skills by attending circle time and participating in the activities.

▲ To help keep the child's attention, use dramatic vocal effects such as whispering, chanting, speaking in contrasting high and low tones, and making funny sound effects with your tongue and lips.

▲ Clap or play a rhythm instrument to accompany children's responses to a listening activity. Let's say that you just read a short story about a dog and now you want the children to tell you what types of pets they like. You might show the children pictures of three or four types of pets, and name them together. Then provide a rhythm by banging on a tambourine as each person in the circle takes a turn choosing her favorite pet and saying, "I like (dog, cat, gerbil, bird, etc.) pets."

▲ Fingerplays need to be simple. Children with developmental delays (and many typically developing children as well) might be able to point their index finger, but have difficulty isolating any of the other fingers. Use fingerplays in which all the fingers work together such as "Grandma's Spectacles" or "Wheels on the Bus," or choose songs that use whole arm and hand movements such as "I'm a Little Teapot" (see words below).

Grandma's Spectacles

These are Grandma's spectacles,
This is Grandma's hat.
This is the way she folds her hands,
And lays them in her lap.

The Wheels on the Bus

The wheels on the bus go round and round,
Round and round, round and round.
The wheels on the bus go round and round,
All through the town.

Other verses:
The people on the bus go up and down.
The doors on the bus go open and shut.
The horn on the bus goes beep, beep, beep.
The wipers on the bus go swish, swish, swish.
The driver on the bus says, "Move on back."
The lights on the bus go on and off.

I'm a Little Teapot

"I'm a Little Teapot" written by Clarence Kelley and George Sanders. Copyright © 1939 Kelman Music Corporation. Copyright renewed 1967 by Marilyn Sanders O'Bradovich. International Copyright Secured. All rights reserved.

I'm a little teapot, short and stout.
Here is my handle,
Here is my spout.
When I get all steamed up, hear me shout.
Just tip me over and pour me out!

▲ Have the children hold hands or hold onto a large hoop, rope, or parachute when doing a movement activity that involves walking around in a circle.

▲ Consider giving each child a paper cup with an appropriate snack to munch on while the teacher is reading or talking. Allowing children to chew on something helps them focus and listen.

▲ It is important to encourage language interaction from those children who are verbal. Pepper your storytelling and reading with questions that require simple one or two word responses.

▲ Hold circle time later in the day when you can talk about what the children have already done that day.

Orthopedic Impairments

Some children with orthopedic impairments are able to participate in circle time independently. A child in a wheelchair who is able to propel the chair by herself can join in many of the movement and music activities, especially those in which the arms are used. On the other hand, this same child might not feel that she is really a part of the circle because she is in a wheelchair and all the other children are sitting on the floor. She is also functioning at a different eye level, so keep this fact in mind when reading books or presenting pictures to the group.

A child with mild cerebral palsy who walks with the aid of crutches or a walker and needs her arms for support cannot easily free them up for movement while she is standing. For this child, incorporate upper body movement games while the group is still seated. You are the best judge of what the children in your group can or cannot do. If you focus on the "can do," you will find that coming up with inclusion activities for the entire group will not be difficult.

▲ Provide seating that is similar to that of the other children. If all the children sit on the floor for circle time, then seat the child with orthopedic impairments on the floor also. It is important for the child to have good support for the head, neck, and trunk so that she can maintain eye contact with the teacher and the other children. Some children will need specially designed corner seats, but others will manage on a beanbag chair or propped against large pillows. A physical or occupational therapist can help determine the appropriate seating support.

▲ Provide seating for all the other children that is similar to the seating of the child in the wheelchair. Have the children and teachers sit in chairs.

▲ If circle time includes movement activities that the child is unable to perform independently, either provide the appropriate assistance or allow the child to perform another function such as turning on the tape recorder or holding a green "go" or red "stop" sign.

▲ Circle time sometimes includes the activity of placing each child's picture tag on a board or placing the appropriate weather cards onto the weather board. Use a movable board and carry it over to the child so that she can also participate in the activity.

▲ Use Velcro or magnetic strips to secure attendance tags or weather cards to the board. The child with poor fine motor control will find these methods easier than clothespins or hooks.

▲ Sometimes during circle time items are passed around the circle for each child to inspect. If the child has functional use of only one arm or hand, place a cushion on the child's lap. The cushion will provide a surface on which the object can be placed without rolling off the lap so that the child can examine it easily with one hand. Encourage the child to use the other hand to hold or assist.

▲ Some children with physical impairments have difficulty turning their bodies

by twisting at the waist. This type of movement is necessary when reaching for objects to the right or left with both hands. When an item is being passed around in circle time, you can easily assist the child by turning her body slightly in the direction of the object. If the child is seated on the floor, simply place your hands on the child's hips and rotate in the appropriate direction. If the child is seated on a chair or in a wheelchair, you can shift her position by turning the chair slightly.

▲ When using rhythm instruments during a music activity, attach bells to an elastic band and place it on the child's wrist or ankle. Other rhythm instruments can be pinned to the child's clothing by tying a piece of cloth to the instrument and securing the cloth to the sleeve, shoulder, or pant leg.

▲ For the child who is non-verbal, ask the parent(s) to tape record something about the child so that it can be shared with the group. The child might be able to participate by holding the tape recorder on her lap and turning it on.

▲ Use a song board from which the child (and the other children too) can select her favorite tune. The child who is not able to point can touch the appropriate picture with any part of her body or even look at the song of her choice. An alternative to a song board is to present each child with two song selections, each one represented by a picture on a large card, and let the child choose between the two.

Pervasive Developmental Disorder (PDD) and Autism

Structure and routine are comforting to the child with autism. Circle time, with its predictable routine, can be a positive experience for this child. On the other hand, circle time might be an overwhelming part of the day for some autistic children because they are being asked to function socially as part of the larger group. The following suggestions are made with the understanding that a wide variety of treatment methods exist for children who have been diagnosed with PDD or autism. Choose and use those interventions that are most consistent with the approach that is used in your school. Also check the suggestions listed in the sections for children with developmental delays and ADHD/behavior issues. Some of those modifications might be appropriate for children with a diagnosis of PDD/autism as well.

▲ Consider making your circle time the same, or nearly the same, every day. Start circle time at the same time of day, incorporating the same songs and activities. You might even want to read the same short book each day for a number of weeks (Maurice Sendak's *Chicken Soup With Rice* is a good choice). Making circle time a familiar daily routine will also benefit other children in your classroom who find comfort in the familiarity of routine.

▲ Allow the child to sit in a rocking chair or beanbag chair. Rocking seems to be an activity that many autistic children initiate themselves to provide comforting sensory input. The pressure of the beanbag chair on the child's body calms and focuses the child.

▲ If an extra adult is available, have her try seating the child on a large ball by holding her securely at the hips and gently bouncing her. This type of movement can help the child with PDD/autism remain calm and better attend to the circle time activity.

▲ Because it may be difficult for some children with PDD/autism to process the stream of verbal information coming from the teacher and

children in a large group setting, consider using this time for a more meaningful activity such as playing in another center with the instructional aide.

▲ Some children seem to respond better to written symbols than to verbal communication. Together with the speech therapist and parents, develop and use symbols, picture icons, or sign language to cue the child for particular circle time activities.

▲ Many children with PDD/autism appear to be highly sensitive to noise. Keep noise levels down. Use quiet music rather than frolicky music, adapt movement activities by making them less rowdy and more controlled, and sing in soft voices or even a whisper. Save rhythm instruments for the outdoors where noise is more easily dissipated.

Attention Deficit/Hyperactivity Disorder (ADHD) and Behavioral Issues

Circle time is frequently a challenging activity for children with attention deficits and other behavior issues. Some three- and four-year-olds who have extremely short attention spans and are easily distracted have not been diagnosed with ADHD because physicians are reluctant to label children at such a young age. After all, many three- and four-year-olds have short attention spans, especially for activities that involve planning and organization, following directions, sitting still, and being quiet. In fact, circle time might be a challenge for many typical children too.

Remember to investigate and try circle time options. We have listed some suggestions in the introduction to this section that include changing circle time to a center choice just like art and blocks are, creating two small circles instead of one large one, and eliminating circle time altogether. We do not advocate any particular approach, but urge you to look at your classroom needs to determine whether the children are benefiting from the traditional circle time arrangement. The suggestions below, as well as those listed in the PDD/Autism section, will help you think about modifications that might work for your circle time.

▲ Seat the child with ADHD next to an adult. Hold the child's hand or simply place your hand on the child's shoulder, back, or leg to help the child focus on the activity.

▲ Seat the child on your lap to provide the direct physical contact that will help the child attend to circle time.

▲ Allow the child to hold a stuffed animal or squeeze a foam ball. This type of activity might provide just enough energy release to help the child stay seated and focused during circle time.

▲ For children who have difficulty sitting still for any length of time, circle time is frequently a battle of wills. Try to adjust your expectations to the child's ability. If you think that the child is only able to attend circle time for one minute, then set a timer for one minute so that the child can be successful on her first attempt. Gradually increase the time, but be careful not to proceed too quickly.

▲ On any given day, environmental factors beyond your control might affect a child's performance. A child might have had a particularly stressful morning at home or on the bus before arriving at school. If you sense that the child is having one of those days, lower your expectations correspondingly. Provide the child with the time and space to calm down while guiding him to appropriate calming activities. Calming activities might include lying in the book corner wrapped in a blanket while looking at books, sitting in the rocking chair while listening to a favorite song with headphones, or sitting inside a tent house or large cardboard quiet "room" while working on puzzles.

▲ For the child who is simply a bundle of energy and cannot sit still, the bus or car ride to school in the morning has already demanded more than enough sitting time. Give this child time to run in the gym or jump on a trampoline in the large motor area before asking her to sit again for circle time.

▲ Consider implementing a consistent reward system for acceptable behavior. This should be done with the advice of a behavioral psychologist or educational specialist who will advise you on how to set up the system, as well as how to phase it out at the appropriate time.

Circle Time

▲ Ignore the negative behavior of the child who is acting up while praising the appropriate behavior of other children. Sometimes this approach results in the improved behavior of all the children in circle time.

▲ Turn-taking is frequently a challenge for the child with ADHD. Impulsivity and distractability cause the child to interrupt other children and the teacher or grab toys that are being passed around the circle. Allow the child to use a fidget toy during this time to help minimize her attempts to grab things from other children. Fidget toys might include squishy balls, twisty snakes, a homemade "squishy," or ball. See page 187 in the appendix for directions for making your own squishy toys.

▲ Offer the child a weighted vest. This is a vest with beanbags or other soft weights placed in front and rear pockets. The deep pressure that this type of vest provides to the shoulders and trunk is frequently calming for the child with ADHD. See page 186 in the appendix for directions on how to make your own weighted vest. Get or make at least two vests that are similar in design, except that one vest has weights while the other does not. Make the vests available to any child in the classroom, perhaps calling them "circle time vests." You will find that the child who needs the deep pressure provided by the weighted vest will usually choose to wear that one. Leave the vests on for a maximum of 10–15 minutes at a time.

▲ Many of the behavior problems that occur during circle time are connected to space ownership issues. Sitting close together during circle time encourages children to touch each other. For some children the touching is accidental and for others it is intentional. One way to minimize this type of interaction from occurring is to seat children at least one foot apart, preferably on their own carpet squares. If you do not have carpet squares, draw circles or squares with chalk or tape to provide each child with a spatial boundary.

▲ Children with ADHD sometimes have difficulty tolerating being touched by others. Their reaction to unexpected touch, especially light touch, might seem quite dramatic to us. This child might hit, kick, bite, or offer nasty verbal remarks because she might interpret even an accidental touch as painful and aggressive. Offer this child a seat next to you. She will feel safer sitting next to a predictable adult than near the more unpredictable children.

▲ Remind children of circle time rules ahead of time. Keep the rules simple and few, but repeat them frequently. The rule can be offered as a positive comment on the children's behavior such as: "I am so pleased that you are all keeping your hands to yourselves during circle time."

▲ Reward desirable behaviors with verbal praise. Offer this type of reinforcement to all the children, not only to those with behavior problems. "You are listening to the story so well," or "You are doing a good job sitting in circle time," are examples of this type of verbal reward.

▲ Some children might misbehave in order to get released from circle time, even if it means being sent to time out. In this case, the child receives attention from the teacher and, even though it is negative attention, it is still rewarding to the child. The best way to deal with this type of situation is by trying to anticipate when the child will not be able to sit through the circle time activity. Instead, you might ask the child to do a special job such as wash and wipe the table for snack time or clean a basket of animal or human figures *before* the negative behavior begins. Physical activity, especially the kind that we might normally call work, can be calming for children with ADHD or related behavioral issues.

Motor Planning Problems

The child with motor planning problems frequently enjoys the listening activities of circle time but might be uncomfortable with the movement portions. These children frequently appear shy and reluctant, especially around new tasks, because they are afraid that they will not be successful. Including children with motor planning issues in circle time will involve a combination of patient understanding of their needs and gentle, but persistent, encouragement of their participation. Trust your instincts to help you judge when to urge a child to try the activity and when to stand back to allow the child to be an observer.

▲ Children with motor planning issues frequently prefer to observe new activities before joining in, especially if those activities involve movement. Allow the child to gain a certain comfort level by giving her enough time to be an observer before expecting even partial participation.

▲ Repeating the same circle time program daily over an extended period of time will give this child the confidence necessary to attempt the group activity. Alter the verbal and visual content to keep circle time interesting, but try to keep the order of activities the same. For instance, a typical circle time might consist of an initial song to bring the children together, weather discussion with appropriate visual props, and sharing the news of the day.

▲ Introduce new activities slowly. Break the task down into its smallest steps, offering extra cues along the way. For instance, if you want the children to side step to the right, demonstrate the movement while you are facing in the same direction as the children. If the children are facing the wall, then stand in front of them and also face the wall. This way, you and the children will have the same spatial orientation. You can help the child discriminate between what the left and right feet are doing by making the initial sliding movement of the right foot soft and quiet, followed by a loud stomp as the left foot closes.

▲ If the child does not respond to your gentle ecouragement to join the movement activity, offer an alternative way to participate. Make a sign or banner that depicts the movement activity that you have chosen and allow all the children to take turns holding it. For the child with motor planning problems, this strategy is a non-threatening way to begin to engage in the group movement activity.

▲ Eliminate unfamiliar motions and replace them with simple daily tasks, such as throwing a ball, washing hands, combing hair, and drinking juice. The familiarity of these activities allows the child to perform the motions spontaneously. As a result, the child is usually more successful because she does not have to plan and organize.

Visual Impairments

Children with visual impairments who are seriously limited in their functional vision use their senses of touch, smell, taste, and hearing to learn about the world around them. Although many circle time activities require active visual participation, circle time can be a wonderful opportunity to offer all the children activities that emphasize the other senses. Feely boxes, musical games, singing, and simple movement games are examples of activities that do not require visual monitoring. We have listed a few suggestions for adapting circle time for the child with visual impairments, but we expect that you will be able to develop many other circle time activities that are appropriate for both the child with visual impairments and the typical child in your program.

▲ Seat the child with impaired vision next to the teacher so that visual material can be viewed from up close.

▲ Accompany all actions and visual activities with clear, short descriptive statements. "Jill is handing the pine cone to Robert so that he can feel it. Then Robert will pass it to Casey." This type of language intervention will also benefit the other children in the group.

▲ If you plan to incorporate a new activity into your circle time, take the child aside prior to circle time and explain the new activity. Also tell the child when to expect this new activity in the circle time sequence.

▲ If children are expected to get their own carpet squares or mats for circle time, make sure that the mat belonging to the child with visual impairment is easily identifiable by color, design, or texture. For the child who is blind, set aside a special spot for the mat so that it can be retrieved independently. For example, hang the mat at the wall near the teacher's seat. This way the child will be able to walk to circle time with the teacher and then find her mat nearby.

▲ Help the child locate her attendance tag independently by placing her attendance tag at eye level.

▲ The attendance tag of a child who is blind should have an easily identifiable texture glued to the back that will help her identify it as her own. Even if the teacher hands the attendance tag to her, she will still be able to verify for herself that it is the correct one. Let the child help choose the texture to place on her attendance tag. Some suggestions include a strip of sandpaper, a piece of satin cloth, or a popsicle stick.

▲ Let the child rest her hands on yours to feel how the hands need to move during song and movement combos. Although sighted children are able to get visual cues about spatial concepts from the teacher or other children, those with severe visual impairments need to experience the meaning of the words in a more concrete way, as when a song says "up, up, up."

▲ Children with severe visual impairments are not able to monitor the position of their bodies in space and frequently demonstrate delayed motor skills and a sense of balance. Keep this in mind when planning circle time movement activities. Movement games and songs that allow the child to keep both feet relatively stationary on the floor will offer a sense of security.

▲ Indicate each child's movement area with a carpet square and modify the marching, skipping, and running activities to marching in place, running in place, and jumping in place. This type of modification can also be done while the children are seated in small chairs, as long as their feet can easily reach the floor. The child will feel more secure knowing that all the children have designated spaces, making the chances of bumping into others or being bumped less likely.

▲ When the child is first introduced to the concept of circle time, it might be helpful to walk the child around the circle of other children before sitting down.

▲ Optimal seating is important for the child with visual impairments. If the child sits close to the teacher, then the teacher can easily offer the child an occasional touch to help her focus on the circle time activity. On the other hand, some children with visual impairments find it beneficial to sit elsewhere in the

circle. Let the child's choice of seating guide you in determining where she should sit.

▲ Give the child an active role to play during story time. She might be able to help hold the book or turn the pages.

▲ Use fingerplays with large movements. Incorporate songs that promote body awareness such as "Head, Shoulders, Knees and Toes." Sing songs that use familiar, functional movements, such as "This is the way." See the words below.

Head, Shoulders, Knees and Toes

Head, shoulders, knees and toes, knees and toes,
Head, shoulders, knees and toes, knees and toes,
And eyes and ears and mouth and nose.
Head, shoulders, knees and toes, knees and toes.

This is the Way

This is the way we brush our hair,
Brush our hair, brush our hair.
This is the way we brush our hair,
So early in the morning.

Other verses:
This is the way we put on our clothes...
This is the way we clean up our room...
This is the way we drink our juice...

▲ Assist with hand and finger movements because the child cannot see them well enough to imitate them.

▲ When you read stories, pass around toy versions of the story characters (such as toy animals or dolls) or use real objects if appropriate (such as carrots, flowers, or acorns).

▲ When discussing the day's weather, let children feel the fabric of a warm winter jacket, a raincoat, etc.

The Inclusive Classroom

▲ Let the child wear a bracelet or ribbon on one arm so that you can give her directions to reach with that hand or the bare hand when items are being passed around during circle time.

▲ When speaking to the group of children, don't stand with your back to the light source. For instance, don't stand in front of a bright window. The glare will make it difficult for the child with a visual impairment to look at you.

▲ Speak to the child in a normal tone of voice. Remember, there is nothing wrong with the child's hearing.

Art Center

The art center is a place for young children to explore the world of scribbles, shapes, designs, and pictures. The suggestions in this chapter will help you include art activities in your daily practice of working with both typical children and children with special needs. This is not a book of new activity ideas, but rather a resource to help you adapt activities you already have planned. We encourage you to continually explore innovative uses of materials for art centers through the many books and guides available at bookstores and through educational catalogs.

Almost every art center activity uses one or more of the following three processes: (1) coloring, drawing, or painting with a tool; (2) gluing, pasting, or taping one or more objects together; and (3) cutting or tearing. Of course a three-year-old will perform these activities differently than a four-and-a-half-year-old, but as long as the art materials are developmentally appropriate, the typically developing child will explore, create, and learn new skills with little direction from the teacher. The child with special needs, however, frequently needs different learning strategies. These strategies require more repetition, teacher direction, and structure. You will find, however, that many ideas, suggestions, and strategies are appropriate for both the typically developing child and the child with special needs. We urge you to trust your own professional judgment when implementing learning strategies with your children. Don't be afraid to try a variety of approaches and don't hesitate to modify our suggestions as needed.

COLORING AND PAINTING

In the art center, children spend most of their time using tools such as crayons, paintbrushes, markers, chalk, stamps, or pencils on a variety of surfaces, the most common of which is paper. Preschool children prefer using markers, followed by chalk, crayon, and pencil, in that order (Brown 1982). Children's artwork begins in the scribble stage. The typically developing child usually explores scribbling between the ages of two and three and a half. Then between the ages of three and five, children begin to draw shapes, starting with straight lines and circles and eventually mastering more complex shapes such as the square and triangle. Finally, they begin to arrange shapes into designs. Typically developing children will move through the art stages with little or no adult instruction, but children with special needs will probably need your help along the way.

Developmental Delays

The child who is functioning at a lower developmental level than his peers might have some skills that are age appropriate and others that are not. Always accept what the child is able to produce at his current developmental level while still trying to move him on to the next stage. Remember that it takes many repetitions for the child with developmental delays to fully learn a new skill. For this reason, some children will appear to have mastered the task one day, but then be unable to perform the same task on another day. This type of inconsistency is common for children with developmental delays, but is frequently misinterpreted as willful misbehavior or laziness.

▲ Encourage the child with developmental delays to participate in open-ended art activities. Use demonstration, task breakdown, and hand-over-hand assistance as needed. Demonstrate the activity by doing it first while the child watches. Task breakdown involves dissecting the activity into small components or steps. Help the child complete one step before going on to the next. Some children will need you to physically guide their hands in addition to the task breakdown and demonstration. This might mean placing a paintbrush in the child's hand and then gently moving the child's hand and paintbrush across a sheet of paper.

▲ For the child with weak hand muscles and a poor grasp, short, stubby writing implements are frequently easier to grasp than commercially available crayons, markers, and brushes. Break chalk, crayon cookies, and chunky (preschool) crayons into short segments, and "fatten up" the handles of markers and brushes. A variety of materials can be used for building up a tool handle. Foam is usually the easiest to obtain. Wrap the thin foam around the handle and tape securely. Other ways to build up paintbrush handles, crayons, pencils, markers, and chalk are (1) insert a short (approximately two-inch or five-centimeter) regular crayon into a Ping Pong ball; (2) cover the ends of an empty yarn cone with cardboard, poke holes through the cardboard, and insert a paintbrush; (3) push a crayon, chalk, or pencil through the opening of an empty thread spool; (4) make your own paintbrush by taping or gluing a sponge on one end of a fat dowel; (5) poke the tool handle through a cylinder of dense, firm foam; (6) wrap a thick elastic band around the base of the handle to make it fatter; and (7) build up the handle with Silly Putty, Theraputty, or firm playdough.

▲ Some children who use an immature, fisted grasp might perform better with thin writing and painting implements. Have a variety of sizes and shapes to meet the individual needs of different children.

▲ Place masking tape, colored tape, or draw colored lines with a permanent marker about one inch (three centimeters) from the brush end to cue the child where to place his fingers.

▲ Encourage the use of an adaptive grasp: place the paintbrush between the pointer and middle fingers and help position the child's hand into a functional grasp as necessary. This adaptive grasp is especially useful when the child displays hand weakness and low endurance for coloring activities.

▲ Add textures and/or fragrances to the paint such as sand, sparkles, and food essence (lemon or vanilla extract) to heighten sensory awareness.

▲ Use a large paper surface for painting to allow for large arm movements associated with less mature developmental levels. Place the paper on a horizontal surface such as a table or the floor, or tape it to a large easel, door, or wall. Be sure to place a large sheet of plastic, such as an old shower curtain or plastic tablecloth, underneath the paper to protect the surface.

▲ Children with developmental delays frequently have difficulty understanding the physical boundaries of their play space. Define the child's art center space by placing the project he is working on inside an old shirt box or on a cookie sheet.

Orthopedic Impairments

The child with orthopedic impairments whose disability affects the upper body, arms, hands, or fingers will benefit from art center modifications. Many commercial aides are available for the child with orthopedic impairments, but this chapter offers inexpensive, easy-to-implement alternatives. Before trying any modification, however, it is important to first make sure that the child is positioned correctly. General positioning guidelines can be found on page 17 in Chapter 1. We also suggest that you consult with the physical or occupational therapist who works with your program.

▲ Some children with physical disabilities prefer using short, fat, writing utensils, while others do better with traditional thin crayons, pencils, markers, and paintbrushes.

▲ For children with limited arm and hand function, tape a piece of paper to the turntable of a children's record player. Then let the child hold a crayon, pencil, or paintbrush against the paper as it rotates.

▲ Use alternative drawing methods that do not involve the use of drawing utensils. For example, place salt or flour over a large sheet of black paper. The child simply needs to move a hand or finger through the salt or flour to create bold black lines.

▲ Make a funnel painter by poking one or two holes in the bottom of a metal or firm plastic container. The child can then move the container across a large sheet of paper to paint.

▲ Stabilize the paper with tape, clips, Fun Tack, clothespins, etc. to prevent excess slippage. At the same time, encourage the child to use his non-dominant hand to hold the paper down. Children with cerebral palsy will benefit greatly from consistent physical and/or verbal cues to use the less functional hand as a stabilizer while painting with the other hand. Another way to secure the paper is to sandwich the paper between a magnetic stick and a cookie sheet. Make the magnetic stick by gluing magnetic tape to a ruler.

▲ Place the paper inside a sturdy shirt-size box that will provide walls to contain extraneous movements of the paintbrush or other coloring tool.

▲ Make a tabletop easel by cutting a sturdy cardboard box on the diagonal. Cut two slits in the top for clothespins to secure the paper.

▲ Use thickened paint to provide more resistance and feedback. Paint can be thickened with cornstarch, salt, sugar, flour, sawdust, or sand. For children with cerebral palsy who have spasticity problems, check to make sure that using more resistant, thicker paint is not contributing to increasing muscle tightness.

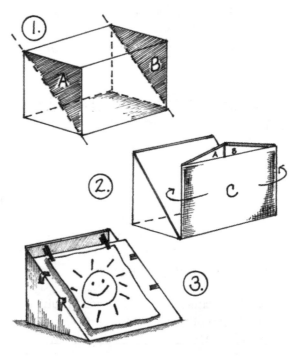

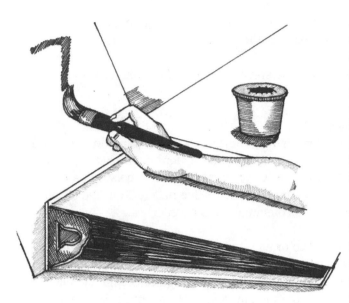

▲ When painting at a vertical or near-vertical surface, provide forearm support by placing an empty three-ring binder under the arm. Use a binder that is four-inches (ten-centimeters) wide or tape two binders together for extra elevation.

▲ Instead of using a table top surface, place the paper on a vertical surface at the child's shoulder level. This position allows the child's head and neck to remain in an upright position that, in turn, makes it easier for the child to visually monitor what he is drawing. This position also helps the child use more mature movement patterns of the hand, arm, and shoulder. Keep in mind, however, that holding the arm up unsupported can be extremely tiring. Allow the child to rest frequently or to return to the project later.

Pervasive Developmental Disorder (PDD) and Autism

Many children with PDD do not like the way many art materials feel or smell. They are already aware of the distinctive odors and textures of crayons, markers, and paints. Be respectful of these differences and do not force the child to use or handle a material that might be unpleasant to him. The type of hypersensitivity is called sensory defensiveness and is discussed in more detail in the appendix on page 183-184.

▲ Chalk, crayons, and paint are materials that are sometimes aversive, but markers are usually acceptable tools for coloring and drawing.

▲ As an alternative to touching fingerpaints or working with poster paints, place thick paint, mustard, or ketchup in a zip-closure baggie. The child then can use his finger or a popsicle stick to draw designs over the surface.

▲ Introduce materials slowly and allow for exploration of materials through senses other than touching; for example, the child might first look and smell, or watch the teacher and other children play with the materials.

▲ Use hand-over-hand assistance to guide the child through an activity. Remember to use firm touch because light touch might feel irritating.

▲ If the child is having a difficult time staying seated, allow him to stand at the art table to work.

▲ Repetitive motions are more conducive to independence than multi-step, complex tasks. Incorporate rhythm, rhyme, and/or cue words (dip and paint, dip and paint…), and try not to use lengthy verbal interactions or instructions. Many of these children respond better to cue words, pictures, or symbols that are written on a piece of paper than to oral directions. See page 188 in the appendix for directions on how to make a communication board.

▲ If the child appears overly active or agitated, try using a calming technique *before* introducing the activity. Slow rocking or swinging is frequently effective. Many children with autism or PDD also enjoy being buried under heavy pillows, beanbag chairs, or mats, or wearing a weighted vest or backpack. See page 18 in Chapter 1 for general guidelines when working with children with autism or PDD.

▲ Use only one or two colors of paint. Brown and black are usually the preferred colors.

▲ Consider using tangible rewards as reinforcement. Consult with a behavior specialist or PDD specialist in order to implement a workable reward system.

Attention Deficit/Hyperactivity Disorder (ADHD) and Behavioral Issues

For many children with ADHD, freeform art activities such as painting, finger-painting, and drawing hold the child's interest for extended periods of time. These children enjoy the opportunity to express themselves in a non-verbal, non-threatening manner.

▲ It might be difficult to transition this child out of an art activity and into another. Use a timer or give the child other cues that indicate the end of the activity. For instance, you might want to use an end-of-playtime song before the clean-up song. The end-of-playtime song gives the child a few minutes to get used to the idea that clean-up time is only a short time away.

▲ State your expectations clearly to the child before he begins the activity. For example, you might state that the child will have fifteen minutes to work on the painting, and you will give him an advance warning when that time is almost up. Also tell the child ahead of time which activity will follow the art center time. Children who are disorganized need frequent information about the day's schedule.

▲ Allow the active child to either stand at the art center table or kneel on a chair. These positions are sometimes easier to maintain than sitting in a chair. If the child prefers to sit, however, make sure that the chair is the appropriate height, with the child's feet flat on the floor. If possible, allow the child to sit in a chair with arms, which will provide additional support and reduce squirming.

▲ Encourage the 4-5 year old child with organizational difficulties to use stencils. Provide stencils that have the basic geometric shapes of circle, square, rectangle, and triangle, as well as stencils that have designs such as leaves, flowers, people, houses, and cars. Tracing a stencil will reduce the frustration that many impulsive children exhibit when attempting to draw a picture freehand.

▲ Sitting, kneeling, and standing are not the only positions that the child with ADHD might use. Lying on the floor while working on an art project is another option. This position allows most of the child's body to come into contact with a hard surface while his body weight is pushing down. In other words, lying on the belly provides the type of pressure touch that can be calming to the active or agitated child. See pages 181-184 in the appendix for a more detailed discussion on the sensory needs of children.

▲ Provide the child with choices as much as possible to reduce the incidence of non-compliant behavior. Offer choices that are acceptable to you, but which give the child the sense that he is in control. For instance, ask the child whether he would like to use a fat paintbrush or a skinny one, the blue paper or the white one.

▲ Children with ADHD are easily upset when their personal space is intruded upon, yet they are eager to invade other people's spaces. Provide an adequate work area with well-defined boundaries. For example, move the easel next to the art table and allow the child to work there alone or place the child's paper onto a cookie sheet at the table. Move the art table against a wall that has been cleared of extraneous clutter so that the child can work with minimal distractions. Or consider making a tabletop "office" from a cardboard box. Cut off the top, bottom, and one side of the box. Cover the remaining three sides with a solid color contact paper and place on the art table.

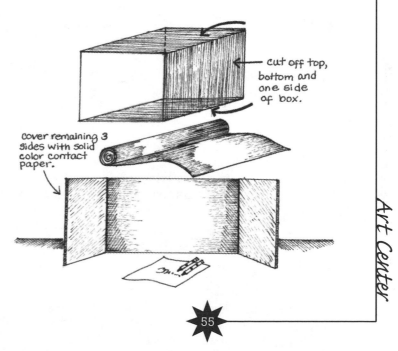

cut off top, bottom and one side of box.

Cover remaining 3 sides with solid color contact paper.

Motor Planning Problems

Children with motor planning problems have difficulty learning new motor tasks and are frequently mistaken as slow learners even though they may have average or above average intelligence. Freeform painting and drawing are generally non-threatening for children who are two and a half or three years old with motor planning problems. The young child is still exploring scribbling and a few basic shapes and is usually not concerned with a product that looks like something. An older child of four or five years, however, might want to draw a recognizable picture and will give up if he cannot produce the intended design.

▲ Break the task down into its smallest steps, demonstrating each step clearly to the child, allowing him to imitate each part until the entire form is completed. Use plenty of verbal cues during instruction.

▲ When drawing a model for the child, position your paper in the same spatial orientation as the child's paper. For example, if the child is painting at an easel, place your paper on an easel too, or tape it to a nearby wall. If the child is drawing at a table, then you should also work on the table surface next to the child.

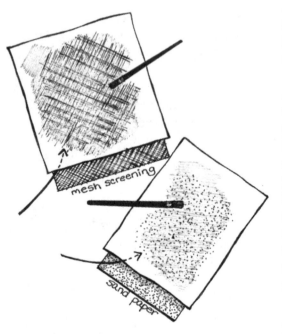

mesh screening

sand paper

▲ The power of peer modeling cannot be underestimated. Position the child next to other children whenever possible.

▲ Encourage the 4–5 year old child with fine motor planning or organizational difficulties to use stencils. Tracing a stencil of a child or a house requires less planning than drawing a freehand picture. Also make available basic shape stencils of circles, squares, triangles, and rectangles, which children can use to provide some structure for their artwork.

▲ Using enhanced sensory feedback is beneficial to the child with motor planning problems. Place sandpaper, mesh screening, or an onion bag under the paper to provide a different texture to the painting surface.

▲ The child with motor planning problems frequently has great difficulty knowing how to begin an activity. If the child wants to draw a picture of himself, for instance, you might need to draw the circle for the head to get him started. Sometimes, drawing only part of the circle is sufficient. Another way to help the child is to draw an imaginary circle over the paper with your finger.

▲ Vary the thickness of the paint by adding sand, sawdust, or cornstarch. You can also change the weight of a paintbrush, pencil, or marker by taping metal nuts or an electronic spacer onto the utensil handle. Make sure that anything you add to the paintbrush or marker does not interfere with the child's grasp.

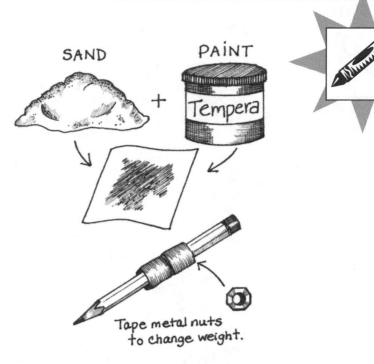

Tape metal nuts to change weight.

Visual Impairments

The child with visual impairments learns about the objects and people around him through the senses of touch, smell, taste, and listening. He is unable to observe and imitate others as they explore the environment and will need help to learn how to investigate the world around him. Offer verbal descriptions about what the room looks like, where furniture and playthings are located, and what other people in the room are doing.

▲ Although some children with visual problems prefer dimmed lighting, most want bright, even lighting. The table surface should have a dull finish on it and be placed in an area of the room where the lighting is optimal to reduce glare and shadows.

▲ Use high-contrast materials, such as dark or bright colors on light paper. Red, yellow, and orange are the easiest colors for a low-vision child to see, especially on a dark blue background.

▲ Place a piece of mesh or screening under the paper when coloring with a crayon so that the child can feel the raised finished product.

▲ To reduce glare from reflection of light, use pastel paper instead of white paper.

Art Center

▲ If a child with visual impairments has never held a crayon or marker before coming to school, you will have to show this child how to hold a crayon or marker and what to do with it.

▲ Hang paper at eye level, either at the easel or taped to the wall. Placing the paper on a vertical allows the child's head and eyes to remain in a neutral position while he is working. It also keeps the picture in the most realistic plane of viewing; for example, if a child wants to draw a tree, the tree will be positioned so that the leaves and branches actually are at the top (closest to the ceiling) and the trunk is at the bottom. Placing that same picture on a table would make the tree look like it was lying flat on the ground. Note that artists usually work at a vertical or inclined surface.

▲ It might be easier to use markers or crayons instead of paint. When using paint, the child has to constantly change his visual orientation as he looks from the paper to the paint and back to the paper. Markers and crayons reduce the amount of visual shifting.

▲ Add enhanced sensory feedback to paint such as thickeners and fragrances. Suggestions include sand, salt, flour, cornstarch, sawdust, lemon juice, vanilla extract, and ground cinnamon.

▲ Remember that doing a visual activity can be extremely fatiguing for a child with visual impairments. Allow extra time to complete projects, encourage frequent breaks, and suggest a low key, relaxing activity to follow.

COLLAGE: WORKING WITH GLUE AND PASTE

Making a collage can be a challenging activity for a young child to plan and organize. First the child has to make some decisions about which materials he wants to use. Then he needs to plan the order in which to glue those materials, decide where to place each collage piece on his project, and, at the same time, manage the physical challenges of gluing—reaching, holding, turning, pouring, and spreading. Many three-year-olds and some four-year-olds will need help mastering the steps of gluing. In general, it is easier to teach children to pour some glue onto the collage base than to spread it on each small collage item. The concept of turning the collage item over so that its sticky side is down is difficult for young children to grasp. White glue is a material that many young children find fascinating. They love to watch it run out of the squeeze bottles and form large white pools on their projects. Although the standard white glue is cheaper to buy initially, glue sticks might be more economical and less wasteful in the long run. And, of course, glue sticks are less messy. Following are suggestions for modifying the gluing and pasting processes for those children who find this type of activity challenging.

Developmental Delays

Children with developmental delays benefit from structured, teacher-directed assistance, consistency, and repetition. Most typically developing children do not need this type of intervention to learn new skills, and, in fact, appear to do better without it. For example, if you want to implement a snow theme for the day, you might put out cotton balls, paper, and scraps of material for a collage activity in the art center. Many of the children will use the cotton balls to represent snow in their collages, but the child with developmental delays might not be able to do so without some extra help. The kind of help that you give will depend on the functional level of the particular child, but it might be as simple as drawing a circle on your paper and gluing lots of cotton balls to make a large snowball. The child with developmental delays might then want to imitate your snowball creation. As a classroom teacher, you will need to balance the needs of the child for structure with the goals of a center-based philosophy.

▲ If the multi-step process of gluing is too complicated for the child, make a collage without glue by using contact paper or another type of sticky collage base. Turn the paper sticky side up and tape it into a cookie sheet or shirt box. The child then only needs to place the collage items onto the sticky surface in order to complete the activity. No glue or tape is needed.

▲ Try not to overwhelm the child with too many choices. Offer only one or two collage materials at a time. Use these materials to teach and reinforce basic concepts by offering appropriate verbal feedback, giving the child information about the materials. For example, "That cotton ball is soft," "What a big piece of red paper you just used!", and so on.

▲ Help the child organize his space by providing small containers for each type of collage material.

▲ Provide the child with a large collage base to compensate for problems with planning the placement of materials and less mature eye-hand coordination.

▲ Use a glue stick instead of the standard white glue for children who have difficulty controlling the amount of glue to pour onto their projects.

▲ Provide clear demonstration as needed, accompanied by short, simple sentences or phrases. Encourage the child to imitate your actions.

Orthopedic Impairments

Collage activities are frequently a favorite of children with orthopedic impairments who have limitations in their arm, hand, and finger control. These children only need to master a crude grasp and release pattern to place collage materials on the paper and feel successful.

▲ Stabilize the base of the collage by taping it to the work surface to prevent slippage. You can also place the collage base on a piece of non-skid shelving material or placemat. Another way to secure a collage base is to clip it onto a tabletop easel with clothespins.

▲ Instead of using a cotton swab or popsicle stick to spread the glue, use a six-inch long fat dowel with a sponge attached to the bottom. It might be easier for a child with a weak or poor grasp to hold onto a fat dowel. Another alternative is to use a fat paintbrush.

▲ Place the glue in an aluminum pie plate that has been taped down to the working surface. The pie plate provides a larger target for children with poor motor control.

▲ Make certain that all the necessary materials are placed within reaching distance. Some children have poor trunk control and lack the ability to fully extend their arms and so are only able to reach short distances.

▲ Because it might be difficult for the child to use refined finger movements to separate small pieces of yarn, cloth, paper, or other collage materials, separate the collage materials ahead of time by placing individual samples of each item on a non-skid surface such as a piece of sandpaper or non-skid shelving material.

▲ Minimize fatigue by reducing the number of steps of the collage process. Use contact paper or precut double-sided tape instead of glue. Pieces of precut tape can be placed along the edge of a plastic container for the child to pull. Weight the plastic container with beanbags or sand so that it doesn't get knocked over.

▲ If the child has severe physical impairments and is only able to complete a collage project with hand-over-hand assistance, consider making better use of this time to practice a more functional skill. An example of such a skill is learning to use switches to activate battery-operated toys or computer activities.

▲ See general positioning recommendations for working with the child with cerebral palsy child on page 17 in Chapter 1.

Pervasive Developmental Disorder (PDD) and Autism

Children with PDD or autism often exhibit heightened sensitivity to materials such as glue and paste. On pages 183-184 in the appendix you will find a more detailed discussion of this behavior, called tactile defensiveness.

▲ Try using contact paper as a base for the collage so that the child does not have to work with glue. The child should be encouraged to simply drop the collage materials onto the sticky paper to avoid touching it.

▲ If the collage project is a more structured, teacher-directed activity such as making a mask, precut the contact paper to the desired shape and place it onto the collage base.

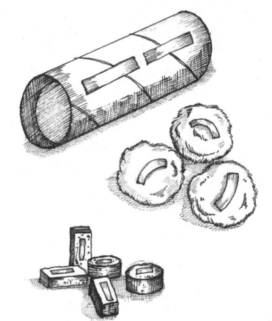

▲ Use large collage materials such as empty toilet paper rolls or large cotton balls. Place precut pieces of rolled tape or double-sided tape onto each collage material so that the child only needs to push the object against the collage base to make it stick.

▲ Some children relate better to written input, recognizable shapes, and simple line drawings. They might be more attentive to a collage activity if they are allowed to glue precut letters, words, and cartoon-type pictures from magazines instead of the usual scrap materials of beads, string, and buttons, etc.

Attention Deficit/Hyperactivity Disorder (ADHD) and Behavioral Issues

Children with ADHD and behavioral issues frequently exhibit poor organizational skills. One child might observe a friend creating a collage of a house and want to make one too. But when he tries, he becomes easily frustrated and quits in despair. This situation results in poor self-esteem for the child and may eventually escalate to anger. It is important to provide this child with the right amount of adult guidance and structure to ensure success.

▲ Have an adult available to sit with the child and guide him through the activity, providing ample praise and frequent feedback at each step of the process.

▲ Do not place all the project materials out on the table at once. The collage materials will distract and confuse children who are impulsive and easily distracted. Set out only the particular material needed for the next step of the activity. When that step is completed, set out the material for the next step, and so forth.

▲ Place each collage material in a separate container and place the child's collage base in a shirt box to help define the workspace.

▲ You might want to move the art table against a wall that has been cleared of extraneous clutter so that the child can work with minimal distractions.

▲ Consider making a tabletop "office" from a cardboard box to help create a more private space. Cut off the top, bottom, and one side of the box. Cover the remaining three sides with a solid color contact paper and place on the art table. See the illustration on page 55.

▲ Modify the collage activity by having an adult complete the initial steps and letting the child put the finishing touches on. He will still consider the collage his very own and feel good about completing the activity "independently."

Motor Planning Problems

The child with motor planning problems relies heavily on visual demonstration, step-by-step task breakdown, and assistance with initiating activities. Frequently these children are keen observers. They prefer to watch the activity rather than participate because, even though they might have a clear idea of what they want to make, they do not know how to go about doing it. Encourage the child with motor planning problems to participate in some aspect of collage making that is non-threatening. Perhaps he could hand you some materials to glue on your collage. Maybe he could choose a collage material and place it on your project.

▲ The child with motor planning issues has difficulty monitoring how hard or how gently his fingers are pushing on the glue bottle. The result is often a massive flood of glue that sometimes finds its way to laps, furniture, and floors. Use thickened glue to enhance the child's sensory feedback so he can monitor how much glue is coming out. It also takes longer for thick glue to come out, giving the child more time to process what is happening and respond appropriately. Thicken glue by adding cornstarch, liquid laundry starch, sand, or flour.

▲ Children with motor planning problems often end up with hands covered in glue because they have difficulty coordinating the grasp, release, and placement of the collage materials. It is important to give these children verbal self-cueing techniques to help them guide their hands and fingers through the motor challenges of the activity. For instance, a verbal cue of "one and done" might help the child shorten the amount of time spent placing glue onto the collage base. A verbal cue such as "pinch and push" might help remind the child to use only the index and thumb to pick up and position each collage piece in place while keeping the other fingers out of the way of the glue. Encourage the child to use similar verbal cues independently.

▲ Often children with motor planning problems have low muscle tone. They might benefit from some vigorous, resistive movement before attempting a more refined task such as gluing. Some suggestions for getting the hands "ready" for gluing are clapping hard and fast, punching a beanbag chair or pillow, doing chair push-ups, crab walking to the art table, or pulling a friend on the scooterboard to the art center. All these activities provide the muscles with exaggerated physical input to prepare them for a fine motor task.

Visual Impairments

Both children who are blind and children with low vision enjoy assembling collages. These children are able to use their heightened sense of touch to guide them through the process and then feel their finished product at the end.

▲ Add yellow food coloring or yellow tempera paint to the glue so it is more easily visible on the collage surface. Use a contrasting dark blue paper for the collage base.

▲ Add sand, sawdust, or other textures to the glue to enhance the tactile feedback.

▲ Use a small squeeze bottle or a commercial glue stick instead of the dip and spread method to avoid lots of mess and spills. Many children with visual impairments have an aversion to sticky materials. Check the suggestions listed in the ADHD and Behavior section for some additional ideas on how to minimize the child's contact with glue and paste while still being able to participate in collage projects.

▲ Place glue in an aluminum pie plate to provide a larger target for dipping the gluing utensil. Place colored tape around the edge of the pie plate to emphasize its boundaries.

▲ Mark the edges of the collage paper with a bright color paint, marker, or tape to help indicate the boundaries.

▲ Line a shallow baking pan with a piece of non-skid shelving material and place the collage materials in the pan.

Art Center

▲ Guide the child's arm and show him where each collage material is located. Be sure to also say what you are doing and describe the position of each item. For example, you might say, "I am moving your hand to the right side of the pan, almost to the edge, to find the buttons."

USING TAPE

Tape is used in many places in the early childhood classroom, including at the art table for constructing collages and at the writing center for sealing envelopes or wrapping packages. Young children like to use tape because it is a grown-up type of activity; however, it is probably a difficult task for most three-year-olds to master. By age four, many children have developed enough finger strength and wrist control to successfully tear tape from a dispenser.

Developmental Delays

The child with developmental delays might find taping a challenge. Does the sticky side go up or down? How do I get the tape off my fingers and onto the paper? How do I line up the edges of the paper and the tape to make it work? Here are some suggestions to help the child with developmental delays be successful when working with tape.

▲ Prepare short, pre-cut strips of tape, about one inch (three centimeters) long. Stick the tape strips onto the edge of a plastic container. You might want to place some beanbags or sand into the container to weight it down so the child will be able to easily pull off a piece of tape without knocking the container over. See the illustration on page 67.

▲ If you want to use a regular tape dispenser, consider taping the entire dispenser to the tabletop with duct tape to prevent it from sliding. Another way to stabilize the tape dispenser is to place it on a piece of non-skid shelving material or rubberized place mat.

▲ Consider using other sticky materials instead of tape: precut pieces of contact paper, self-sticking labels, or a variety of sticky tabs and "buttons" that can often be acquired at a recycling center. Using these alternative "tapes" requires the child to peel them off a backing, but it still might be less complicated for some children than tearing tape from a dispenser.

▲ Use contact paper for the base of the collage. Tape the contact paper to the table, sticky side up, so the child can simply drop the collage materials onto it.

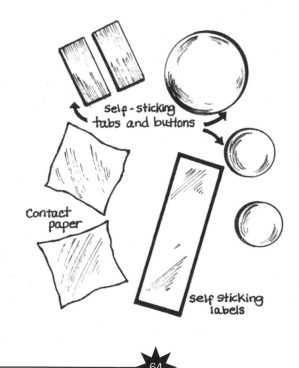

self-sticking tabs and buttons

Contact paper

self sticking labels

▲ Use other types of tape such as colored electrical tape and masking tape. It is easier to distinguish between the sticky and non-sticky sides of these tapes.

Orthopedic Impairments

The child with orthopedic problems might have difficulty working with tape because of the fine motor dexterity that it requires, especially when the tape gets stuck to fingers. Although we include some suggestions for modifications, it might be easier for the child with orthopedic impairments to use contact paper or glue.

▲ Stabilize the tape dispenser by taping it to the table with duct tape or place it on a piece of non-skid shelving material or rubberized place mat. In this way the child can tear the tape using one hand only.

▲ Prepare short, pre-cut strips of tape, about one inch (three centimeters) long. Stick the tape strips onto the edge of a plastic container that has been weighted down with beanbags or sand. This way the child will be able to pull a piece of tape off using one hand only. See the illustration on page 67.

▲ Use double-sided tape to reduce the frustration of manipulating regular tape to the proper orientation. Make your own double-sided tape by rolling precut pieces of masking tape, sticky side out, and attaching the ends together.

▲ Use Fun Tack instead of tape.

Pervasive Developmental Disorder (PDD) and Autism

Children with PDD or autism frequently do not like working with sticky materials such as tape. Do not try to guide this child through a taping activity with hand-over-hand assistance, as you might with other activities, because the child might become quite agitated. Use the same caution when dealing with other materials that you suspect are irritating to the child.

▲ Place pieces of double-sided tape onto the collage surface so that the child is able to place the collage materials onto the tape without touching the tape at all. If appropriate, let the child show you where to place the tape.

▲ Use contact paper for the base of the collage. Tape the contact paper to the table, sticky side up, so the child can simply drop the collage materials onto it.

▲ Consult an occupational therapist about using appropriate desensitization techniques before presenting sticky activities.

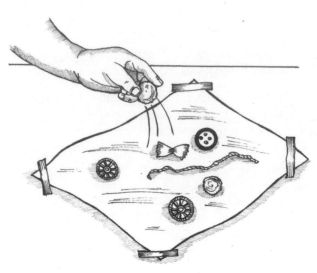

▲ Provide a calming activity for the child before using tape. Calming activities include rocking in a rocking chair; wrapping up in a blanket; and lying under a mat, beanbag chair, or other soft, heavy item.

▲ Since eye contact sometimes improves when the child is lying on his back, secure the taping activity to the underside of a table or chair and allow the child to work while lying underneath the piece of furniture. Make sure to use duct tape or another strong tape to secure the collage base. Also test the materials that will be used to make sure that they will easily stick to the tape. Tissue paper and other lightweight papers and fabrics are preferable to heavier items such as buttons and lids.

Attention Deficit/Hyperactivity Disorder (ADHD) and Behavioral Issues

For children who tend to be impulsive, using tape might be a frustrating experience. Tape easily tangles, sticking to itself or to undesirable surfaces when handled by young children who are not carefully monitoring what their hands and fingers are doing. Also, some children with ADHD, like some children with PDD, do not enjoy handling sticky materials. Please check the suggestions for children with developmental delays and PDD or autism to see if any might be appropriate for children with attention and behavior issues.

▲ Consider using other sticky materials instead of tape such as precut pieces of contact paper, self-sticking labels, or a variety of sticky tabs and "buttons" that can often be acquired at a recycling center. Using these alternative "tapes" requires children to peel off a backing that might also be frustrating for those with poor fine motor skills.

▲ Prepare short, pre-cut strips of tape and stick them onto the edge of a plastic container. Place beanbags or sand into the container to weight it down so the child will be able to pull off a piece of tape without knocking the container over.

Motor Planning Problems

The child with motor planning problems relies heavily on visual demonstration, step by step task breakdown, and assistance when initiating activities. Frequently these children are keen observers. They prefer to watch the activity rather than participate because, even though they might have a clear idea of what they want to make, they do not know how to go about doing it.

▲ Reduce the number of steps by eliminating the tearing of the tape. Place pre-cut tape strips on the table or along the edge of a weighted container.

▲ Place an "X" or other simple mark on the non-sticky side of each piece of masking tape to indicate which side of the tape needs to be facing up. If the child can see the "X," then the tape has been positioned correctly.

▲ Many children with motor planning problems rely on using trial-and-error techniques to figure out how to do a new task. For children who will probably need to move the tape from one spot to another on their project before they get it right, use plastic, metal, wallpaper, shelving paper, or other types of non-stick surfaces instead of paper for the collage base.

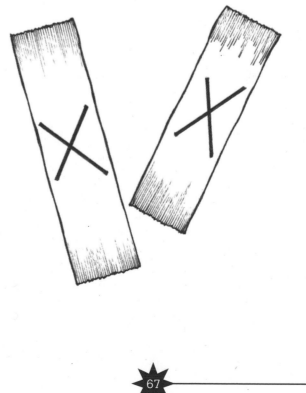

▲ Offer simple verbal cues to guide the child through the taping activity. The child might then be able to use the same words to cue himself the next time he uses tape. Instead of saying the cue words out loud, remind the child that he can use his silent voice.

Visual Impairments

Taping activities can be frustrating for any young child, but especially for a child with visual impairments. Use your own judgment to decide whether to make tape available in your classroom.

▲ Use double-sided tape. The child can place a strip of double-sided tape onto the collage surface and then simply press a piece of collage material onto the tape.

▲ Mark the outside edge of pre-cut tape strips with an "X" to encourage children with low vision to see which side of the tape to stick to the paper.

▲ Use high contrast tape such as colored masking or electrical tape. Eliminate clear or transparent tapes.

▲ Unlike gluing, taping projects can be done at a vertical surface. Consider fastening the base of the collage to an easel or wall at eye level to make it easier for the child to see.

▲ Offer the child lots of verbal information about what the collage project looks like: "you are putting that piece of tape near the edge of the paper...now you have two buttons in the middle and three cotton balls under them...your collage is full of circles and stars."

CUTTING WITH SCISSORS

Young children love to use scissors even though learning to use scissors is quite a challenging experience for them. Many three-year-olds will sit for long periods of time snipping scraps of paper, doing a better job than a paper shredder. Some four-year-olds might begin to show interest in cutting out shapes, but other children continue to have difficulty despite all their efforts. Many three-year-olds are simply not developmentally ready to handle the complicated task of cutting. You have probably noticed that many young children hold their forearms inverted with the scissors pointing down when trying to cut. Although this arm position looks awkward to us, it works for the child as it provides the shoulder and wrist stability necessary for handling scissors. Although children are not required to master cutting with scissors before they are allowed to "graduate" to kindergarten, they should not get into the habit of using immature arm positions. Here are some suggestions to help all children practice cutting skills while providing the kind of support they still need.

The following modifications assume that the child has shown the desire to learn how to cut with scissors and has demonstrated the necessary developmental skills that make mastery of scissors a reasonable goal. An occupational therapist can help you determine if a child is ready to learn how to cut with scissors.

▲ Make sure that children are seated in small chairs so that their feet rest flat on the floor. Encourage them to rest their elbows on the table when using scissors to give them extra support for their upper body.

▲ Provide them with thin strips of heavy weight paper, such as greeting cards that have been precut into one-inch (three-centimeter) strips, to practice snipping.

▲ Encourage other activities that help prepare the large and small muscles for using scissors: digging in the sand, pulling a wagon, pushing a friend in a cardboard box, assembling nuts and bolts, hammering pegs, and, of course, tearing. Most freeform art activities can be easily modified to use tearing instead of cutting with scissors.

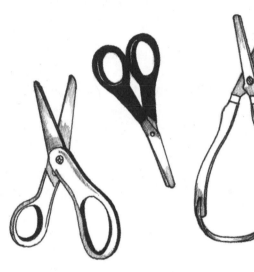

▲ Some scissors are better than others, especially for little hands. Using the right scissors might make the difference between success and failure for your three- and four-year-olds. We suggest using scissors that are small, sharp, and clean. Refer to page 190 in the appendix for a complete listing of commercially available scissors. Most scissors should be replaced every two to three years because they become dull and covered with glue.

▲ The correct finger position for holding scissors is with the thumb in one loop and the middle (tall) finger in the other loop. Place the index finger on the outside of the scissors blade to stabilize the scissors. When cutting, the forearm should be in a neutral position. This position is the same as you would use when shaking hands with someone, with the thumb facing the ceiling.

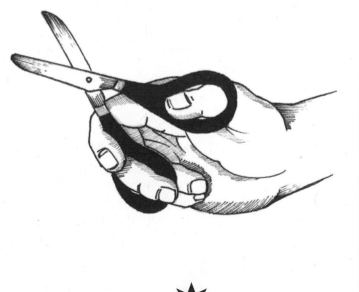

▲ Frequent hand switching is observed during cutting activities. For many children, hand switching is simply an attempt to improve their performance: if the right hand is having a difficult time, maybe the left one will do better and vice versa. For some children hand switching might indicate fatigue, motor planning prob-

lems, midline crossing issues, or, simply, a yet undeveloped hand dominance. Although the underlying reasons for hand switching will vary from one child to the next, here are some general guidelines for addressing ongoing hand switching during cutting activities:

✓ If you notice the child switching hands, suggest to the child that he put the scissors down for a short break. Maybe you and the child can count to ten together or say a jingle such as, "These scissors need to rest a bit. On the table let them sit. Two, four, six, eight, ten, now they're ready to cut again." Frequently the child will return to the hand that he had been using initially.

✓ Observe which hand the child uses for eating, coloring, pointing, etc. If you can determine an obvious preference for one hand over the other, then you might be able to encourage the child to use the identified dominant hand for cutting also. Gentle cues such as, "Let's teach this hand how to use the scissors first. Then we'll teach the other hand later."

✓ If the child is left-handed and has already begun to demonstrate mastery of cutting with his right hand, then leave well enough alone. This child has simply learned to adapt to the right-handed world in which he lives.

✓ Constant hand switching might be an indication that this child is not developmentally ready for cutting. Put the scissors away and try again in a couple of months. In the meantime, encourage the use of two hands for activities such as stringing beads, assembling Legos, hammering and cutting playdough, and assembling nuts and bolts.

Developmental Delays

Remember that the developmental age of this child will place him at a younger functional level than other children and will certainly affect his readiness for cutting with scissors. Scissor skills are difficult for most preschoolers to master, and are especially difficult for children with developmental delays. Many children with developmental delays also have low muscle tone that affects their ability to hold the scissors firmly.

▲ Encourage the use of tearing. Tearing is a wonderful way to build up hand and finger muscles as well as promote the development of left-right coordination.

▲ Encourage the child to snip short, thin strips of paper. Do not expect the child to cut out a shape or even cut along a straight line.

▲ Use strips of heavyweight paper such as oak tag, cookie and cracker boxes, wallpaper, and old greeting cards. Unless you are using children's sharp Fiskar scissors, children will have an easier time cutting paper that has some firmness to it and won't collapse between the blades.

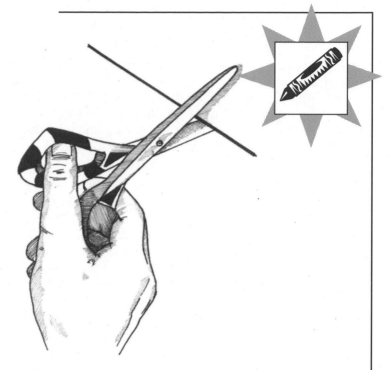

▲ If the child insists on using scissors, provide the necessary guidance for thumb and finger placement. Use scissors whose handle loops are different colors or wrap a piece of colored electrical tape around one loop. Try to have the child place his thumb in the same colored loop each time he uses the scissors.

▲ Use a variety of weighted and textured papers to enhance sensory feedback. Sandpaper and wallpaper are good for this purpose. Cut other materials such as straws, aluminum foil, and playdough to offer the child different sensory information.

▲ Give verbal cues and use words that are meaningful to the child. Instead of saying "open and shut," you might say, "Open the scissor's mouth and take a bite of paper...mmm...yummy. Now let's take another bite."

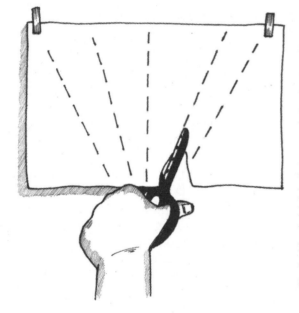

▲ Tape the paper to a wall to practice cutting along a vertical line. This paper position encourages correct orientation of the child's arm, with the scissors and thumb pointing up toward the ceiling.

▲ Wrap tape around the loops to make them smaller for little hands. The bulk of the tape helps teach children to do continuous, smooth cutting because it prevents the scissors from closing all the way with each snip.

Orthopedic Impairments

When a child with moderate or severe physical impairments is unable to use scissors independently, an adult or another child should offer him the help he needs. Provide as much or as little assistance as necessary. For some children, this help might mean cutting the entire project for them, while other children might only need assistance to hold and turn the paper.

▲ For the child who has the functional use of only one hand, consider taping the top edge of the paper to the table or wall so the child can cut lines and simple shapes independently. It is still important to remind the child to use his less functional hand as best as he can to help stabilize the paper.

▲ When using regular children's scissors, try wrapping tape (Coban tape works well because it sticks to itself) around the loops to make the holes smaller. The bulk of the tape also prevents the scissors from closing all the way, helping to approximate a more natural, continuous cutting stroke.

▲ Try different types of scissors. Spring-loaded, self-opening scissors and loop scissors require less fine motor control than regular scissors, while certain small scissors such as Benbow scissors are perfect for young, immature hands. Benbow scissors are available through some therapy catalogues (see page 190 in the appendix). Battery-operated scissors are also an option but should be used only with close adult supervision.

▲ Cutting is a difficult task and can be especially tiring for children with physical disabilities. Provide extra time to complete the activity and encourage frequent rest breaks. The child might also need a few minutes of "recuperation" time at the end of the activity.

Pervasive Developmental Disorder (PDD) and Autism

Cutting with scissors is a skill that is mainly used for school work in kindergarten and the primary grades. Older children and adults generally use scissors only to snip thread or string and to cut on straight lines for wrapping paper or newspaper coupons. So our suggestion for children with moderate to severe PDD or autism is to put scissor skills in perspective and focus instead on teaching the more essential life skills of self-care and communication.

▲ Some children who have PDD or autism and are high-functioning will be able to learn how to cut with scissors, but might occasionally use the scissors inappropriately, especially when they get caught up in perseverative behaviors such as snipping off tiny pieces of paper. Redirect the child or help him stop the pattern by giving the scissors a rest for a few minutes.

▲ Structure the cutting experience by drawing short lines along the edge of the paper so that the child will use repetitive short cuts to make a fringe.

▲ Children with PDD or autism who are attracted to letters and words might be encouraged to practice functional cutting by cutting out specific words or letters from a magazine to match words that you have already placed on the paper.

▲ Use scissors with different colored handles. Different colors might help the child remember that the thumb fits in the "blue loop" and the middle finger in the "white loop."

▲ Use a variety of weighted and textured papers to enhance sensory feedback. Sandpaper and wallpaper are good for this purpose. Cutting other materials such as straws, aluminum foil, and playdough will also offer the child important sensory information.

▲ Offer the child help with turning the paper for more complex tasks such as cutting curved lines, circles, and squares.

▲ Cutting with scissors requires sustained, controlled eye contact. It might be easier for the child to maintain the necessary visual attention when lying on the floor on his back. This position appears to facilitate visual gaze.

Attention Deficit/Hyperactivity Disorder (ADHD) and Behavioral Issues

Impulsivity, short attention span, and distractibility do not lend themselves to easy mastery of scissor skills. These children will need plenty of adult guidance and encouragement to become successful at cutting with scissors. Careful adult monitoring will also be important because of the safety concerns you might have with giving scissors to children who behave in unpredictable ways.

▲ A child who is out of control and is holding a pair of scissors is probably not what you want to have in your classroom. Be sure to provide this child with the necessary structure and limits before the activity begins.

▲ Try to reduce the frustration factor for this child by providing activities at which the child can be successful or by offering assistance. The child might feel less overwhelmed by the activity if he knew he only had to complete the final few snips of the project. This type of adult assistance is preferable to having the child become frustrated and possibly throwing a tantrum in the middle of the activity.

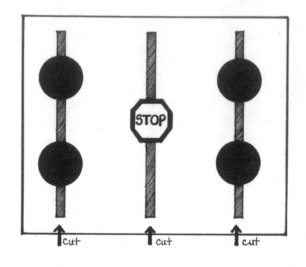

▲ Identify the child's space with some type of physical boundary such as a placemat or small hoop. Make sure that the cutting area is not too crowded with children and/or objects.

▲ Offer the child the choice of sitting at a separate desk next to the larger art table. This arrangement will give the child a sense of space while still being part of the art center.

▲ To help the child learn to cut slowly and accurately, draw red dots, circles or "STOP" signs every couple of inches along the path to be cut. This might also help the child stay visually in touch with the activity as his eyes move from one "STOP" sign to the next.

▲ Superimpose colored marker segments over the line that is to be cut. For instance, the first segment could be purple, then red, blue, green, etc. The child will now view this activity as a series of attainable short steps, rather than one large, overwhelming, project.

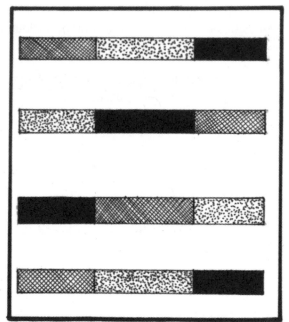

▲ Many pre-drawn forms and stencils for cutting have narrow lines to delineate the cutting boundary. Use a wide-tip, colored marker to make the boundaries bold and wide. A width of one-quarter inch is appropriate for preschool ages, but can even be exaggerated to three-eighths inch or one-half inch for children who need more obvious visual cues.

Motor Planning Problems

Learning how to use scissors is frequently one of the most frustrating experiences for the young child with motor planning problems. Cutting with scissors is a complex task for all young children, but is especially difficult for children with motor planning issues.

▲ Break the task down so that each step can be mastered one at a time. Allow the child to describe to you what he is doing so that you will be able to use those same cue words later to help the child remember how to approach the task.

▲ Use scissors with different colored loop handles. It might be easier for the child to remember that the thumb always fits in the "blue loop" and the middle finger in the "white loop."

▲ Help children remember which fingers to place in the scissor loops by placing a consistent mark on the thumb and middle finger. For instance, you might offer all children a small blue star sticker to put on the thumb and a small white one for the middle finger to match the colors of the scissor loops. Or you might have special finger rings available for the children made from pipe cleaners or rubber washers that would be placed on the middle finger before beginning a cutting activity.

▲ Use a variety of weighted and textured papers to enhance sensory feedback. Sandpaper and wallpaper are good for this purpose. Non-paper materials such as straws, aluminum foil, and playdough will also offer the child important sensory information. The child can roll the playdough into a long carrot and snip off pieces for "carrot soup."

▲ Help reduce the child's frustration by offering to help turn the paper for more complex tasks such as cutting curved lines, circles, and squares. Then have the child help you turn your paper when you are cutting.

▲ Tape paper to a wall to practice cutting along a vertical line. This paper position encourages the child to hold his arm in the correct position with the scissors and thumb pointing up toward the ceiling.

▲ To help the child guide the scissors, draw red "STOP" signs every few inches along the path to be cut. Each stop sign is a target at which the child can aim his scissors, making this activity a collection of small cutting tasks rather than one big overwhelming project. See an illustration of this on page 74.

▲ Superimpose colored marker segments over the line that is to be cut. For instance, the first segment could be purple, the next red, then blue, green, etc. The child can now approach this activity as a series of shorter tasks, with the purple segment as the first cutting task, then the red as the next, and so forth. See an illustration of this on page 74.

Visual Impairments

The child with visual impairments may want to learn how to use scissors just like the other children. Teaching this child how to use a new complicated tool will probably be challenging, especially because many children with visual impairments have not explored their environment enough to adequately develop their hand and finger muscles. Provide as many opportunities as possible for safe exploration and always encourage children to use as much of their vision as possible.

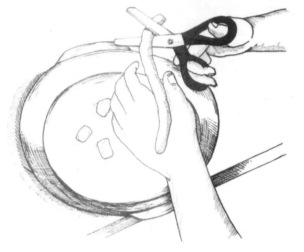

▲ Cutting with scissors is not a functional activity for children who are blind. They should instead be encouraged to work on more functional skills such as buttoning. For children with some vision, cutting would be more appropriate.

▲ Snipping a plastic straw or a playdough "snake" is an appropriate cutting activity that requires only one scissor "bite" at a time. Let the cut pieces fall into an aluminum pie plate so the child can hear what he is doing. Encourage him to practice cutting one-inch (three-centimeter) strips of paper. Gradually provide wider strips of paper to encourage two and three "bite" cutting.

▲ Use a wide black, red, or orange marker to exaggerate the boundaries of the form that is to be cut.

▲ Outline the boundary that is to be cut with white glue. You can add food coloring to the glue to make it more visible. When the glue is completely dry, it will provide a hard, raised surface to help the child guide the scissors.

▲ Place strips of masking tape along the boundary of the form that is to be cut. Cutting through the double thickness of paper and tape provides extra tactile and kinesthetic cues for the child with visual impairments.

▲ It might be easier for a child with a visual impairment to see what he is cutting if the paper is taped to the wall at his eye level.

▲ Provide plenty of verbal information about what the child is doing and what the project looks like.

Sand and Water Center

Sand and water is always a favorite center and is often full of children busily sifting, pouring, scooping, and shaking. Children love sand and water and will play with it for an extended period of time, experiencing concepts of big and small, rough and smooth, full and empty, fast and slow. This center is a place for active play where children develop fine motor and sensory motor skills. Children also practice language skills as they plan and negotiate at the sand and water table.

One problem with the sand and water table is that it provides a limited space for play. Children don't have as much flexibility about positioning themselves in relationship to other children as they would in another center, such as blocks. Therefore, the sand table is potentially more stimulating and may result in more conflicts between children, which can interfere with constructive play. The number of children at the table, and the amount and kinds of play equipment offered, should be adjusted to the arousal levels of the children who will be at the sand and water table.

The location and stability of the table is an important issue in the inclusion classroom. Often the sand and water table is on wheels, making it an unstable piece of play equipment for children with motor difficulties. To reduce unnecessary distractions and stimulation, position the sand and water table out of the main traffic pattern in the classroom.

Vary the materials used in the sand and water table. Flour, salt, dirt, water with food coloring, sawdust, small smooth pebbles, large buttons, snow, or Easter basket grass are examples of materials that can be used instead of sand or water. Any of these materials can result in spills and a dirty classroom floor; many also present a choking hazard and need to be carefully supervised. To minimize the inevitable messes, place a plastic tablecloth or shower curtain under the sand and water table.

Young children may not want to make anything in particular, but prefer to explore the sensory properties of sand and water. They may do the same action repeatedly, such as squeezing a sponge filled with water. The two-year-old, or a child who is functioning at the two-year level, may have difficulty sharing or following safety rules and may need more adult supervision. At the two-year level, the child learns best through observation and imitation.

Three-year-old children have developed more dexterity and can pick up small objects with their fingers. They are able to play more independently and use words to describe color, shape, size, and quantity. Four-year-olds are beginning to interact and play with other children. Their play is more purposeful. The four-year-old child can classify and sort items by size, shape, and color.

Children who are five and older are able to role-play while playing with sand or water. They can follow three-step directions, and their play with other children is more cooperative, with improved respect for the property of others (Miller 1994).

Equipment recommended for sand and water play:

eyedroppers	basters
tongs	water pumps
sand shovels	sifters
scoops	coffee measures
spoons	squirt bottles
food coloring	sand and water table
shape molds	cookies cutters
water wheels	spoons
basins or dishpans	funnels
egg beater	clear plastic tubing
plastic boats	plastic people
plastic animals	plastic plates and utensils
egg cartons	film canisters
ice cube trays	hollow balls
toy boats	wooden beads and blocks
combs	bubbles and blowers
spray bottles	toy bulldozers and dump trucks
popsicle sticks	dry tempera paint

cups and containers, various sizes
containers with screw-on caps, preferable translucent plastic
sponges cut into small squares
corks and other materials that float
cloths and scrub brushes for washing items
containers with small holes punched in the bottom

SAND TABLE

Sand can be eaten or thrown, so for safety sake, keep an eye on children when they are playing with sand and instruct them how to play with sand safely. Comment on what the children are doing when they are playing. Encourage children to use language to describe what they are doing and to communicate with peers. If the sand table is on wheels, check to see if the wheels can be removed or place the sand table next to a wall to prevent rolling.

General Suggestions

▲ Regulate the number of children at the sand table based on the ability of the children playing to tolerate jostling and distractions.

▲ The height of the sand table should be adjusted so children can play in an upright position with both hands able to reach the sand.

▲ Initially provide sand toys at the child's current level of skill. Gradually introduce more advanced play skills.

▲ Put out just a few pieces of equipment; rotate with new equipment from time to time.

▲ If sand seems to be too overstimulating, replace with a heavier material such as small pebbles, although these might be a choking hazard if the children are not carefully supervised.

▲ Place basins of sand in the sand table if children are having difficulty staying in their own space. Basins of sand can be placed on a child's wheelchair tray if the chair is unable to fit under the sand table.

▲ Encourage children to use language skills when playing in the sand.

Developmental Delays

The child's skills may be a year or two behind that of the typically developing children in the classroom. This child needs time to play at her current level of skill and would benefit from having more mature play skills broken down into manageable steps. For example, if the child is able to scoop and pour sand with her hand, give her a shovel and offer physical assistance to shovel sand into a bucket. Gradually phase out hand-over-hand assistance as the child learns the skill.

▲ If the child is distractible, she will benefit from having a small group at the sand table, perhaps just one other role model. The stimulation from the sand and too many other children jostling for sand toys can overwhelm the child with developmental delays.

▲ Match the activities to the child's level of skill. For example, the severely delayed child will benefit from filling and pouring, burying objects in the sand, or stirring powdered tempera paint into the sand with a spoon (Granovetter and James 1989). The child with more mature fine motor skills could search for hidden objects in the sand, fill plastic turkey basters with water and squirt the water into the sand, or pack sand into containers to build castles or other structures.

▲ Give clear directions in small steps. Although the typically developing child may not require explicit directions for sand play, the child with developmental delays may need to expand her repertoire of play behaviors. The child may get caught up in the sensory aspects of play, such as running the sand through her fingers, and not progress to using sand toys or functional play without adult guidance.

▲ Model language concepts such as big, small, full, and empty while the child is playing in sand.

Orthopedic Impairments

If the child is positioned well, playing with sand can help to improve her muscle tone and coordination. Encourage independent movements rather than hand-over-hand guidance during sand play.

▲ Position the child at the sand table to promote functional movement. If the child spends her day in a wheelchair, and the water table is stable, sand play might be a good time for use of equipment such as the prone stander. This option should be reviewed with the physical or occupational therapist. To encourage independent play, the child's head should be positioned at midline and the trunk should be symmetrical; the child should not be leaning to one side. Both hands should be positioned at midline, or one hand can be weight bearing or holding the play materials while the other hand manipulates the objects. The goal is to have the child actively involved in reaching, grasping, and using sand toys.

▲ We have observed that children with tight muscles sometimes have difficulty tolerating tactile input and may have a strong impulse to withdraw from the sand. Gradually introduce the sand. Often firm touch such as pressing hands firmly into the sand is easier for the child to tolerate than lighter touch such as trickling sand on the child's arms. If the child is having difficulty with the tactile input from the sand, encourage her to use sand toys, such as shovels, instead of touching the sand.

▲ Most sand tables are too low for a wheelchair to be positioned close enough for play. If the child cannot be positioned to play functionally at the sand table, a container with sand and toys can be placed on the tray of the child's wheelchair. It is important to invite a peer role model or partner (another child in the class) to play as well.

▲ The child will benefit from having times during the day to get out of her wheelchair and stretch her muscles. Placing the child on her belly on a wedge with a dishpan of sand and sand toys on the floor in front of her is a great opportunity for play out of the wheelchair, especially if a peer partner is included. Be ready to try another position such as sitting in your lap if the child is unable to play actively in prone position.

▲ If the child is not using verbal language, provide pictures of the various sand toys so that the child can indicate a choice. If the child does not respond to pictures, hold up two sand toys and have the child indicate a choice by pointing.

Pervasive Developmental Disorder (PDD) and Autism

This child may be reluctant to use sand toys in a purposeful way and may prefer sensory activities such as repetitively sprinkling the sand. Use pictures of sand activities and repeated practice with sand toys to help the child to be comfortable with sand play.

▲ Sand play may be overstimulating for the child who is overly sensitive to touch. Replacing the sand with large smooth pebbles can be easier for the child to tolerate because the pebbles are heavier and give firmer touch input. Pebbles lend themselves to many scooping and pouring activities. Because small pebbles present a choking hazard, use only large pebbles.

Sand and Water Center

▲ Although the number of peer role models (other children in the class) at the sand table should be limited to one or two children in order to control touch and auditory input, encourage the social interactions of sharing and turn taking for the child with PDD.

▲ If the child seems to be stuck in repetitive, self-stimulatory play with the sand or sand toys, demonstrate more functional use of toys and gradually phase out physical prompts as the child uses toys more meaningfully.

▲ Children who refuse to try activities at the sand table may be more comfortable if they include a favorite, motivating object in the play. For example, if the child is interested in trains, she should be encouraged to push the train through the sand. Gradually encourage the child to try some of the less familiar sand toys and phase out the use of the train.

▲ If the child seems very anxious about touching the sand, break down the experience into very small steps. First the child can stand near the sand table, then later the child can touch the sand table, followed by touching a sand toy, eventually touching the sand with a shovel or toy and gradually touching the sand.

▲ If the child becomes overstimulated by sand play, a weighted vest may help the child to feel calmer. Please refer to page 186 for information about making a weighted vest. Add or take away weights every ten minutes or take the vest off after twenty minutes so that the child's nervous system doesn't get used to the weight and therefore the vest loses its calming effect.

Attention Deficit Hyperactivity Disorder (ADHD) and Behavioral Issues

These children may need a structured sand experience. Offer a few toys and model how you would like them to be used. Children with attention disorders tend to flit from center to center. Use a timer to encourage the child to stay at one center for gradually longer periods of time in order to practice new skills.

▲ Carefully monitor the child's level of arousal. If the child seems to be overreacting to the sand play with increased activity or out of control behavior, redirect the child to a quieter center or to the quiet area described on page 185 in the appendix. Sometimes the child can be overstimulated, but look very unfocused and underresponsive. The child may "shut down" to protect her immature nervous system from an overload of sensory input. The child who is overstimulated would benefit from slow rocking, time in the quiet area with a blanket, or a firm backrub.

▲ Large pebbles or buttons in the sand table may be easier for the child with tactile defensiveness to tolerate because they are heavier and provide firmer sensory input. Watch to make sure children are not putting these items in their mouths because of the potential for choking. Provide an appropriate alternative object to chew on, such as a piece of aquarium tubing, if the child is mouthing objects.

▲ The child should clearly understand the rules and consequences of negative behavior. For example, throwing sand will result in time out. Praise appropriate play at the sand table.

▲ Observe the events that precede negative behavior. Consider factors such as the texture of the sand or being crowded by other children as possibly contributing to the child's undesirable behaviors. By carefully observing what is happening around the child's behaviors, more effective interventions can be planned.

▲ Assess whether what looks like negative behavior might possibly be overstimulation. The child may be in an overaroused state from play with the sand or close contact with the other children and might act out as a result. This child might be helped to cope more comfortably with this experience by modifying her sensory diet as described in the appendix on page 182.

▲ Give the child only one or two sand toys such as a funnel and a scoop. Any other child at the sand table should have a similar set of sand toys. After a few minutes, when the child's attention span wanes, exchange the toys for two others.

▲ Instead of using one large sand table, consider placing dishpans or other basins inside the sand table so that the child will have a defined space for sand play.

▲ Wet the sand with warm water. Moistened sand might feel less irritating than dry sand to the child with ADHD who is easily overstimulated by tactile input. On the other hand, sticky wet sand may upset some children. Experiment to see what is best for the individual child.

▲ If respecting other children's personal space at the sand table seems to be a problem, give the children rug squares to stand on.

Motor Planning Problems

Encourage these children to come up with their own plans for sand play and to verbalize them to you. Describe what you see the child doing in a positive manner. "Great job pushing the sand with the toy truck." Be specific about what you see the child doing rather than giving general praise such as, "Nice job!"

▲ Sometimes, children with motor planning problems have low muscle tone and might benefit from proprioceptive input from jumping on a trampoline before tasks that require maintaining an upright posture, such as standing at the sand table.

▲ Weighted vests (see page 186) can give the child proprioceptive input that helps with trunk stability and awareness of self in space. Add or take away weights every ten minutes so that the child doesn't get used to the weight.

▲ Encourage the child to plan what she is going to do at the sand table and to verbalize the plan. After the child has attempted to carry out her plan for sand play, review with the child whether or not the plan was successful.

▲ The child with motor planning problems would benefit from attempting to follow simple directions given by an adult or another child. Demonstrate the action if needed, such as filling a sand mold and dumping it out to make a cake. Pair actions with an easy-to-remember verbal cue, "Fill and dump!" Encourage the child to say the phrase with you.

▲ Encourage the child to observe peer partners for play strategies at the sand table.

Visual Impairments

The sand table is an excellent opportunity for the child with visual impairments to learn to use touch and vision to explore and talk to the child about everything that is in the sand table and what the other children are doing at the sand table.

▲ Position the sand table in a well-lighted area of the classroom.

▲ Review with the child what toys and equipment are in the sand table. Only use a few toys at a time in the sand table.

▲ Give frequent verbal cues and physical prompts when introducing sand table activities. Gradually reduce prompts to facilitate independence. Leave the same toys in the sand table until the child has mastered their use.

▲ Make available sand toys that have auditory feedback such as sand wheels and sifters.

▲ Use brightly colored toys to contrast with the sand. Red, orange, and yellow are especially good. You can modify less colorful sand toys by accenting with strips of colored tape. For example, place tape on the handle of a shovel or the rim of a bucket.

▲ If the child is unwilling to put her hands in the sand, she can place her hands on top of yours and experience moving her hands through sand and using sand toys.

▲ Smooth large round pebbles may be easier for the child to tolerate than sand. See the illustration on page 83.

▲ Encourage the child to listen to and identify sounds at the sand table such as the scrape of the shovel in the sand or the sound of sand being dumped into a bucket.

WATER TABLE

Water fascinates and relaxes most children. Add bubbles and equipment for pouring, and watch the play unfold. Sponges, eyedroppers, and basters not only move water, but also help to make hands stronger. To prevent the spread of germs, children should wash their hands before playing in the water table and the water should be emptied each day. Spray the tub and toys with a diluted bleach solution of one part bleach to ten parts of water after each use.

General Suggestions

▲ Supplement verbal directions with demonstrations and picture symbols when instructing children with language delays in the use of water toys.

▲ Observe the child to determine if the level of stimulation at the water table is comfortable. If the child is focused on the water play and interacting with the other children, the amount of stimulation is probably at an optimal level.

▲ Introduce novel water toys when the child's attention begins to fade.

▲ Provide turkeys basters and eyedroppers in the water table to work on hand skills.

▲ Place the water table in a well-lighted, visually non-distracting area of the room.

Developmental Delays

Make sure the children have opportunities to play at their ability level. Children will benefit from experiences where they can try new skills that have been broken down into manageable steps.

▲ Start by giving the child simple one-step directions such as, "Scoop the water." Add a second step only when the child is able to respond to one-step directions.

▲ Observe to see if skills learned in similar activities such as the sand table are generalized to water play. Practice and reinforce the same basic skills, for example, "in" and "out."

▲ Structure the situation to encourage interaction with other children. For example, have children pour small cups of water into a larger communal bucket.

▲ In order to cue the child to listen to verbal instructions, position yourself at the water table so you can maintain eye contact with the child.

▲ If the child is not yet using verbal language, use pictures for the child to indicate choices of toys or to demonstrate the sequence of an activity.

▲ Instruct the child in how to imitate actions at the water table.

Orthopedic Impairments

Water play can be a good opportunity for the child to play actively. Children often find water fun and interesting. When the child is interested in reaching and playing, you will find it easier to encourage active, independent movements.

▲ When a child spends much of her day in a wheelchair, water play can be an excellent time for a position change. The child can lay on a wedge, with both hands in a dish basin of water. Water temperature can influence muscle tone. Warm water has a more relaxing effect on tight muscles. Children with mild motor problems can kneel at a low table to play with water.

▲ The child should be encouraged to actively use water toys, not just splash in the water or be passively moved hand over hand. Try to give as little help as possible, perhaps just supporting the child's elbow so she can use her hand to play.

▲ If the child does not have verbal language skills, use a communication board (poster board with pictures of the centers on them) for the child to indicate choice of activities, such as water table or housekeeping center.

▲ Experiment with the size of shovels or scoops until you find one that is easiest for the child to manipulate when scooping water. Provide a variety of toys to encourage the child to adapt to different play experiences.

▲ Introduce a cup like the one the child drinks from at snack for water play (a two-handled cup works well) so that the child can practice holding and using

the cup to pour. Be sure the child understands that the cup is for playing, not for drinking, at this time.

▲ Incorporate language concepts such as" full and empty," or "float and sink" into the water play.

Pervasive Developmental Disorder (PDD) and Autism

Water play is typically an interesting and enjoyable activity for children with PDD. This is a time to encourage language skills, by keeping language input simple and consistent. Name what the child is doing, such as "Pour!" and repeat that phrase as the child performs the activity.

▲ Almost all children love water play. If the child dislikes water, allow the child to participate in another activity. Provide pictures that the child can use to communicate another choice.

▲ Use water play as a time to teach social skills, such as giving a toy to another child or taking a toy if one has been offered. Set up the situation so that the child has to say or do something to make things happen. Facilitate the play interaction between the two children.

▲ Observe the child at the water play table. If the child seems relaxed, makes eye contact with the other children, and plays functionally, then the stimulation is just right. If the child is crying, has eyes averted, or is attempting to bolt from the water table, the activity is probably too stimulating and the activity should be modified. Try providing the child with a small basin of water to determine if she can play more comfortably without the jostling of the other children. Perhaps the water temperature is uncomfortable for the child and she might be better able to play if the water was warm or at room temperature. Sometimes limiting the number of toys in the water table can make the experience more manageable for the child.

▲ It is important for children with autism and PDD to be able to anticipate what comes next in a center. For example, use verbal or visual cues to show the child that first there will be some washing and rinsing of the baby doll in the water, then drying. It is helpful to use visual cues, such as picture icons, to give the child a sense of the sequence of activities.

▲ Sometimes pairing actions to a song helps the child with PDD focus on the tasks. For example, when washing a doll you might sing, "This is the way we wash the baby, wash the baby, wash the baby. This is the way we wash the baby, so early in the morning," sung to the tune of "Here We Go Round the Mulberry Bush."

▲ If the child seems frightened of water play because she is unfamiliar with the activity, introduce water play gradually. Have the child stand near the water table for a minute or two, watching the other children play. After the child can tolerate being near the water table, have the child touch the table, followed by touching some of the water toys and eventually touching the water. If introduction to the water table is carried out in small steps, it will be less stressful for the child.

Attention Deficit Hyperactivity Disorder (ADHD) and Behavioral Disorders

The child may find water play a preferred activity and play quietly and with interest. Conversely, the open-ended nature of water play may be too unstructured. Observe the child's play and intervene if necessary to move the child to another center.

▲ Be clear about behavioral expectations for this center and be firm with consequences if the child does not comply with rules for the water table. For example, give time out for splashing water.

▲ Group the child with a small number of peer role models (other children in the class) who will demonstrate functional play skills.

▲ Introduce novel water toys when the child's attention begins to fade, perhaps offering the child an eyedropper to wash or "feed" small plastic animals in the water table.

Motor Planning Problems

Water play does not require complex motor planning and may be a comfortable activity for the child with motor planning difficulties. If the child seems ready, this might be a successful center for the child to make plans with other children for water play.

▲ Verbalize the steps the child will need to follow in water activities. Encourage a peer partner to demonstrate the activity for the child.

▲ Use heavier water toys, utensils, and dishes in the water table to give the child more proprioceptive input and increase the ability to motor plan.

▲ Encourage the child to slow down and do one step at a time.

▲ If the child seems to be invading others' space, give her a rug square to stand on. This helps the child to have a sense of her personal boundaries.

Visual Impairments

It is important that the child feels she is having an effect on her environment. The child needs to manipulate objects to identify them and to explore the water table to find toys. You can pick up cues about how interested a child is in a water toy by how eagerly she explores it and whether or not she searches for the toy if it falls (Davidson and Nesker Simmons 1992).

▲ Look for water toys that have a contrasting color and will be easier to visually locate in the water table.

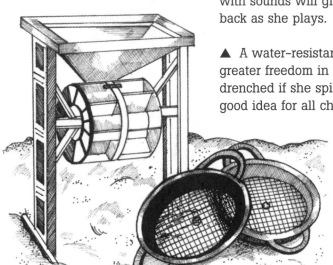

▲ Water wheels that click or other water toys with sounds will give the child auditory feedback as she plays.

▲ A water-resistant apron will allow the child greater freedom in play without getting drenched if she spills water on herself. This is a good idea for all children at the water table!

Block Center

5

Blocks come in a variety of materials, shapes, and sizes and offer a wonderful opportunity for young children to explore imaginary play and to learn the planning and organizational skills associated with the construction of buildings, roads, and bridges. Children can play alone or in small groups, each one working at his current developmental level.

Two-year-olds enjoy stacking blocks in tall towers, then knocking them down. They also line up the blocks on the floor and experiment with carrying heavy loads of blocks around. Three-year-olds begin to build structures such as simple bridges and enclosures, but like the two-year-olds, prefer to play alone. By age four, many children incorporate imaginary play into their block building to include people, animals, and cars. Their block building is more complex, involving patterns and symmetry, bridges, and multifunction constructions. For five-year-olds and older, block play can become an elaborate enterprise that includes sharing and cooperating with other children to carefully plan intricate structures.

Many children with special needs play in the block center successfully without any modifications simply because blocks lend themselves to such a variety of developmental levels. Other children, however, might benefit from environmental adaptations and teacher intervention to help them structure their block play into a meaningful and rewarding experience. Although we have listed our suggestions according to special needs categories, you might find that a modification listed in one category will also work for a child in a different category. Check the suggestions for developmentally delayed children when considering changes for a child with pervasive developmental disorder (PDD), autism, or behavioral issues. Check suggestions under the orthopedically impaired section when looking for possible modifications for a child who is visually impaired.

One frequently mentioned suggestion for the block center is to provide designated play spaces for individual children. Many children benefit from having physical boundaries for their play, as well as knowing where other children's spaces are. Defining a child's block building area with a carpet square, a taped-down piece of shower curtain, or a section of particle board is easy to implement. Encourage children to build on their own section of special floor, singly or in pairs. Some children might even need a well-defined building space, such as the inside of a large refrigerator box or an empty plastic children's pool.

Place a basket of blocks at each block building space. Having the blocks nearby prevents many inadvertent block structure crashes as children go in search of more blocks from the shelves or from other children's piles. A basket of blocks for every one or two children also allows the teacher to have some control over

the types of blocks that children use. Some children are ready for and need many blocks with a variety of shapes and sizes. Other children, including those with moderate and severe developmental delays, pervasive developmental disorder (PDD), autism, and visual impairments, usually do better with a limited number and type of blocks.

Developmental Delays

The child with developmental delays frequently is not ready to use blocks in fantasy play as many typically developing children are. Some might simply enjoy carrying blocks around as they explore weights and textures while others prefer placing blocks into a container and dumping them out again. Occasionally, these children use blocks in ways that might hurt themselves or others. They might mouth, chew, or throw blocks, or knock down block structures that other children have been working on. We hope that some of the following suggestions will prevent these behaviors from occurring as you help these children play appropriately in the block area.

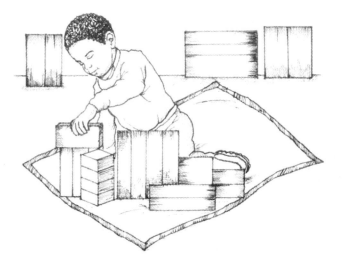

▲ Define a space within the block area center by having the child work on a special "floor." This area can be defined by spreading an old sheet, shower curtain, or other suitable material on the block center carpet. Cut or fold the material to the desired size and tape the corners down to prevent it from rumpling or being pulled. Invite one other child to play in this special space.

▲ Place a preset number of blocks into a large container next to the child so the child does not have to repeatedly return to the shelves for more blocks, potentially crashing into other children's structures on the way.

▲ Allow the child to play with only a small number of blocks (five to eight) initially. Use blocks that are the same size and shape, then gradually introduce new shapes and sizes, as the child becomes familiar with appropriate block play.

▲ Although block play is unstructured and can accommodate many developmental levels, children with cognitive delays frequently benefit from additional props to facilitate the imaginative use of blocks. Place toy human figures, ani-

mals, cars, or road signs in the block area to encourage the child with developmental delays to create block structures and play for longer periods of time.

▲ If mouthing or throwing blocks is a problem, consider using non-toxic plastic blocks instead of wooden unit blocks. Soft, hollow, plastic blocks are easy to wash and are less destructive if thrown.

▲ Discourage chewing on blocks by offering appropriate substitutes. Allow the child to carry a fanny pack with appropriate mouthing toys. Items that you might put in the fanny pack include non-toxic plastic tubing, and straws for chewing, and a variety of whistle and blow toys for blowing on. Check page 189 in the appendix for specific fanny pack suggestions.

▲ This child benefits from more teacher direction than you might provide for typically developing children. Model appropriate block play. Build a ramp and slide a car down while making engine sound effects to interest the child in block play. Stack two blocks and knock them down. Then encourage the child to do the same.

▲ For children who are severely delayed, modeling of block play needs to be developmentally appropriate. You might need to model placing blocks into a container or banging two blocks together in order for the child to be interested and successful.

▲ Give the child lots of positive encouragement. He needs this type of support and encouragement not only to attempt new activities, but also to repeat and practice the skills he has almost mastered.

▲ If this child has difficulty with transitions, be sure to give sufficient advance warnings for clean-up time.

▲ Make available a variety of block sizes, including one-inch (three-centimeter) cubes. Provide opportunities for the child to imitate your block designs and practice visual-perceptual and hand-dexterity skills.

▲ Encourage children to play with blocks in a variety of positions such as lying on their bellies, on hands and knees, or kneeling. Playing in these positions will help develop strength and stability in the trunk, neck, shoulder, and arms.

Block Center

Orthopedic Impairments

The child with orthopedic impairments might have the cognitive and perceptual skills to construct elaborate structures with blocks but is unable do so due to physical limitations. Block center modifications for this child will focus on modifying the environment to promote the most efficient use of the child's arms and hands.

▲ Consult with an occupational or physical therapist in order to arrange optimum positioning for the child in the block area. Correct seating will allow the child to interact with the blocks and with other children in the most independent manner possible. One option might be to place children on their bellies on a wedge-shaped mat on the floor. They can also lie on the floor with a small bolster under the chest. This position offers the child with orthopedic impairments support for the upper body while leaving the arms free for block play.

▲ Some children need the trunk support of a floor sitter. Make your own seat by sawing the legs off a child-size chair. Tie a large scarf or belt around the child's waist and chair for extra security.

▲ Small blocks can be manipulated with one hand while large blocks require two hands for manipulation. Use small blocks for a child whose orthopedic impairment limits or prevents the functional assistance of one hand.

▲ Blocks that snap or push together such as preschool Legos or Bristle Blocks can be easily modified for a child with one functional hand. Build a base from the blocks, then secure the base by taping it to the table, wheelchair tray, or floor. To construct a Lego base, you will have to use two layers of blocks. The blocks of the second layer have to be positioned perpendicular to the first layer in order to lock the bottom layer into place. Bristle Blocks can be secured to each other end to end so you will only need one layer to form a stable base.

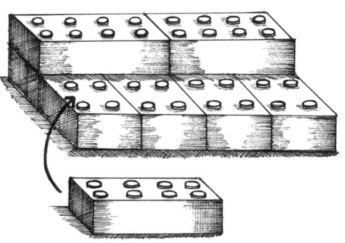

▲ Grasping, lifting, and assembling blocks might cause the child to tire quickly and become fatigued for the remainder of the day. Be alert for signs of fatigue and offer sufficient breaks.

▲ Have the child build against a wall or other flat surface. The wall acts as a physical guide for accurate block placement and provides extra support for the structure after the blocks are stacked. If there is no bare wall available, use the side of a weighted cardboard box or the back of a bookshelf.

▲ Independent block play can be frustrating for children with poor balance, trunk control, and eye-hand coordination. Consider pairing a child with orthopedic impairments with another child to form an assembly line. The role of the physically challenged child might be to pick up the block and hand it to the other child or it might be simply to point to the block that comes next. You might be able to think of additional ways to incorporate this type of cooperative play idea into your block center.

Pervasive Developmental Disorder (PDD) and Autism

The child with pervasive developmental disorder or autism can be highly sensitive to one or more types of sensory input. In the block area, the unexpected noise of blocks falling against each other or onto the floor can be frightening, disorienting, and even painful. Although children with PDD or autism are not offended by the texture of most blocks, the specific odors that some blocks, especially plastic ones, give off might be quite offensive. Most of us do not even notice these odors, but these children are frequently painfully sensitive to smell, especially if the odors remind them of a previous negative experience. Between the noise and the smells, the block center might not seem like a safe play area from the child's point of view.

Some of the suggestions in the ADHD and Behavior section are also appropriate for children with PDD or autism. We mention them again here with a slightly different focus that emphasizes the unique characteristics of these children. Remember that the general suggestions mentioned in Chapter 1 on page 19, such as using a soft, calm voice and making available a quiet "room" like a large refrigerator box, are important and should be implemented throughout the entire day.

▲ The child with PDD or autism might not choose to play in the block center because he is afraid of the blocks crashing and causing an unbearable noise. Respect the child's feelings and do not force him into an area when there is obvious resistance. Gradually, have the child move closer to the block center, first standing near it to watch other children, then sitting in the center touching a block, and finally picking up a block.

▲ Provide the child with the opportunity to play with blocks in another area of the room that seems "safe" to the child. This safe area might be inside a large box that the child is already familiar with as a haven away from visual and auditory stimuli. Make sure that the floor of the box is well padded to minimize the noise of falling blocks.

▲ Cardboard blocks fall more quietly than wooden or plastic blocks, but they still produce hollow thuds, especially when crashing onto a bare floor. Use flat pile rugs on the floor to cut down on unnecessary noise.

▲ Choose a day to put out foam blocks instead of unit blocks. Allow only two children to play at any one time, keeping the noise level and commotion down to a minimum.

▲ Use pictures to communicate. Show the child a picture of a block structure or a child building with blocks. Then whisper to the child, "You build too."

▲ Sometimes counting as the child builds a tower with blocks helps the child stay focused on the activity.

Attention Deficit/Hyperactivity Disorder (ADHD) and Behavioral Issues

The child with ADHD or behavioral issues frequently finds block play a calming activity. Using the large muscles to lift and carry heavy materials provides the child with sensory feedback to the muscles, tendons, and joints that helps him to relax and focus. The block area can also become a place for fighting over materials and space as children who are impulsive and easily distracted move about the area to gather more blocks, bumping into other children or block structures. The following suggestions are intended to help you set up the block center space to minimize conflict for children who are impulsive, distractable, disorganized, or have territorial issues.

▲ Define the child's space within the block area by providing the child with a special "floor." This might be an old sheet, a shower curtain, or another suitable material. Cut or fold to desired size, and tape the corners down to prevent the special "floor" from being rumpled and pulled.

▲ Define children's spaces by marking boundaries with solid color tape. If there is enough room, provide an area for each child. If space is limited, let two children share the building area. You could also identify the space by placing a card with the child's picture or name in each area.

▲ Place a rug in the block area to cut down on the noise levels of crashing blocks. Use rugs with non-skid backs and flat pile, such as indoor-outdoor varieties. Individual rugs or mats are also an option. The rug has to be large enough to house only the block structure, not both the structure and the child.

▲ To minimize intrusions into other children's spaces, provide each child with a large basket of blocks. This way, children do not have to return to the shelves for more blocks, potentially crashing into other children's structures on the way.

▲ Have one or two consistent rules for the block area such as "only touch your own blocks and your own structure." Repeat the rules frequently to the children who are playing in the block area.

▲ When the children play appropriately, be sure to tell them so. They need frequent verbal feedback to learn what types of play are considered appropriate.

▲ Provide props for imaginative play to help the child play for a longer time. Let the child gather the props before starting block play by giving him choices. "Do you want the horse and cow or the cat and dog? The car or the truck? The blue scarf or the green?" Letting the child make these choices will help reduce power struggles.

▲ A child with impulsive and disorganized behavior might have difficulty stacking blocks accurately, resulting in a wobbly, insecure structure that keeps falling down. For a child who already has a low opinion of himself, only one failed attempt might make him angry enough to throw or kick the blocks. To prevent this type of behavior, you will need to intervene before the child even begins to play in the block center. Explain to the child that blocks sometimes have a hard time staying where you put them. Then remind the child to come and get you as soon as he notices that the blocks are not "behaving." You might have to remind him a few more times while he is playing.

▲ Wooden block structures should never be built higher than the children's heads so they do not seriously hurt anyone when falling down.

Motor Planning Problems

Children with motor planning problems find playing with blocks a non-threatening activity. Blocks can be assembled in a variety of ways and lend themselves to many developmental levels of play. Children with motor planning problems may have average or even above average cognitive ability yet they have difficulty planning and carrying out motor tasks. For instance, a four-year-old child with motor planning problems might be able to identify squares and rectangles, tell you which books are squares and which are rectangles, and might even know that these shapes have four sides. But the same child might not be able to easily organize the blocks on the floor to form even the simplest shapes. Fortunately, blocks are very forgiving. The child can manipulate the blocks as much as he wants until he succeeds. This type of trial-and-error problem solving is one way the child with motor planning problems learns. Unlike crayons and markers that leave permanent marks on paper, blocks are a natural trial-and-error material.

▲ Offer the child with motor planning problems encouragement and praise as he works his way through the trial-and-error process of creating with blocks.

▲ As the child is playing, offer verbal descriptions and information about the process. For instance, if the child has put four blocks together to form a rectangular enclosure, you might say, "That looks like a rectangle with two small blocks facing this way and two long blocks facing the other way." These types of clues might help the child remember how to reproduce the same structure a second and third time.

▲ Imitation is a beneficial learning tool for all children and especially for children with motor planning problems. Ask the child to help you build two houses, one for each of two dolls or plastic animals. You build one simple structure and encourage the child to build the other.

▲ Encourage children with motor planning problems to play with one or two other children. Watching how other children assemble block structures will give the child with motor planning problems visual information about the steps of the process—which block comes first, which comes second, etc.

▲ If the child seems hesitant to even attempt independent block play, first try to get him interested in what you are building. Perhaps he could bring you some blocks or some props. After the child feels comfortable at that level of play, ask him to add a couple blocks to your structure. Maybe he could make a wall a little taller or make a driveway leading up to the door. Gradually help the child gain confidence in his ability to succeed in block play.

▲ Encourage building with blocks of various sizes and weights. Small blocks facilitate hand dexterity while large, heavy blocks provide more sensory feedback to the joints and muscles.

▲ Have the child build against a wall or other flat surface. The wall acts as a physical guide for accurate block placement and provides extra support for the structure after the blocks are stacked. If there is no bare wall available, use the side of a weighted cardboard box or the back of a bookshelf.

Visual Impairments

Both the child with partial sight and the child who is blind enjoy playing with blocks. The child who is blind initially will have no idea what to do with blocks and will need your assistance to explore some completed structures before he is able to tower blocks and build independently.

▲ Initially, give the child with visual impairments only a few blocks. This child needs the opportunity to explore the new shapes, weights, and surfaces before engaging in more advanced block play.

▲ Place the blocks in a basket or wagon that can be positioned close to the child.

▲ Have the child build against a wall or other flat surface. The wall acts as a physical guide for accurate block placement and provides extra support for the structure after the blocks are stacked. If there is no bare wall available, use the side of a weighted cardboard box or the back of a bookshelf.

▲ The child with visual impairments can help put the blocks away if the storage shelves are marked with raised templates instead of pictures. You can make templates by tracing each block shape onto cardboard or sandpaper, cutting the shapes, and taping them to the shelves. The child can feel the template shapes and match the blocks to the appropriate shelf.

▲ Demonstrate how to build horizontally with unit blocks so that most of the blocks are in contact with the floor.

▲ Use interlocking blocks such as Legos or Bristle Blocks instead of unit blocks.

▲ Use a contrasting color for a building surface. If the child is using wooden blocks and you already have a blue or red rug in your block area, then the problem is solved. However, if the blocks are used on a wooden floor, consider placing a primary colored thin mat or rug on the floor for the child to use during block play.

▲ Tape strips of sandpaper onto the sides of wooden blocks to provide a non-skid surface.

▲ Place adhesive Velcro on block surfaces to help the blocks stick together.

Dramatic Play

6

We can mean a variety of things when we say we want children to play. Perhaps we want children to practice their social language and interpersonal skills through playful interaction with other children. Play can also be used as a format for children to improve gross or fine motor skills. Sometimes when we talk about play, we mean that joyful, self-initiated activity that all children and adults need to have as part of their lives. In all of these kinds of activities, we find that some children with special needs require assistance to develop their ability to play.

We should provide playful environments and experiences for children based on their needs. The best way to assess these needs is to observe children playing (Fisher, Murray, and Bundy 1991). Modifications can then be made to the toys and materials used in play, the play environment, the play activity, the position of the child, the way in which children play together, or the expectations of what the child is able to do. We know that play is important to the child's cognitive, language, and social development, yet it can be very difficult to find the time to model play behaviors when so many other activities are going on in the classroom that require your involvement. It is a temptation to leave children on their own, because play is something many children can do independently. However, both typically developing children and children with special needs may have difficulty playing constructively and creatively. They may need help to expand their play strategies. To do this, you could could play with the children, or ask specialists such as the occupational or speech therapist to spend more time in the classroom on play skills. Instructional aides or parent volunteers are another valuable resource to assist the children in developing play skills.

In their book *Pathways to Play*, Heidemann and Hewitt offer excellent information about the stages of play and how to help children develop play skills. The child's first play experiences involve exploring the uses of objects. Only one object is manipulated at a time. The child may fill containers or dump objects. Next, comes simple means/ends play. The child is beginning to play with toys, such as busy boxes or see-and-say toys, in which pushing a button or pulling a string makes something else happen. This stage is followed by organized constructive play. The child uses formboards, puzzles, and other toys that require visual perceptual skills. The child then develops functional use of objects. During this stage, the child utilizes common objects, such as a spoon, cup, brush, or phone without pretending. The child may have a tendency to favor a toy or play activity that she uses repeatedly. Play is largely non-verbal at this stage, but it contributes to language development if the adult labels and describes what the child is doing. The child's play at this level may not involve other children. The child may learn from watching other children without including herself in group play or may play alongside other children in parallel

play. These play behaviors are typically seen in two-year-olds.

After the child has explored the properties of objects, she progresses to pretend play. The child uses common objects to act out familiar activities. Sometimes it is evident that a child is pretending, like when she blows out imaginary birthday candles or makes slurping noises when sipping imaginary tea. If the child is not using real objects to pretend, you will need to demonstrate the use of real objects for pretend play. For example, you could give the child a doll and baby bottle and model feeding the doll.

Next, the child uses common objects to engage in play directed toward dolls or stuffed animals. For example, the child will pretend to care for a stuffed animal by feeding it a bottle and putting it to bed. This is followed by representational play with a toy being manipulated by the child to do something with an object, such as pretending that a stuffed animal or doll blows out the candles on a birthday cake. Typically at this stage one action is performed at a time. There is no linking of one play activity to another, although the child may direct one pretend action toward different toys. For example, the child may brush a stuffed dog, a doll's hair, and a plastic zebra. Later, two or more pretend actions are performed successively. In this kind of play, the child may feed an action figure and then brush its teeth. The child begins to interact with other children in her role and there is more use of language. The child with language delays may need instruction in how to talk with other children during play. You may need to say, "Ann, tell Sarah that the baby is hungry and needs some food." These play schemes are emerging in three-year-olds.

The child will next play with combinations of play activities, successively performing two or more pretend actions that have a relationship. For example, a child may pour imaginary juice from a pitcher and begin to drink. By age four, objects are then used to represent a missing object. The child may use a block to represent a bed. If the child is not using objects symbolically, you might collect objects that are similar to the real object and suggest how the substitute objects can by used. For example, you could hand the child a block and say, "You can pretend this is cake. Feed this cake to the baby."

The use of substitute objects is typically followed by the use of imaginary objects. Again, you may first need to demonstrate imaginary play, such as sweeping the floor with an imaginary broom. Heidemann and Hewitt suggest the use of songs such as "Wheels on the Bus" with imaginary actions.

This stage is followed by role play. The child first takes on the role of familiar people such as mother or father. Four-year-olds pretend to be less familiar people such as doctors or firefighters, followed by even more unfamiliar roles, such as astronaut or pilot. Some children may need time to observe this kind of play before joining in, or they may need to practice this kind of play with an adult before participating with other children. Interesting props will support role play.

Five-year-olds and older children have complex play. The child begins to plan, organize, and negotiate with other children to coordinate the play. This play is

cooperative, goal-orientated, and often directed by one or two children. A play theme might continue over a period of days and involve lots of discussion with other children. Interaction between children can be facilitated by play in small groups, teaching children to say a child's name when addressing her, and responding to the comments of other children.

Anita Bundy explores some other important issues involved with play in the book, *Sensory Integration*. Play should involve intrinsic motivation—the child should want to do the activity for the fun of doing it, not because someone has told her to. Children should have a sense of control and feel that they can do whatever they want with the toys and play activities. Play should be absorbing and elicit active involvement. There should be more interest in the process than the product. Real play may not look like what we think of as play and may be disorganized or include some risk-taking. We need to be aware of the difference between play and social skills training and include both when working with special needs preschoolers (Fisher, Murray, and Bundy 1991).

The following suggestions are designed to include children with special needs in the dramatic play centers. While observing children in this center, take note of how the child is playing. Play checklists, such as the one developed by Heidemann and Hewitt, can be helpful when observing or evaluating children's play.

Please keep in mind that we are not suggesting that you carry out all of these adaptations for any child or group of children. You may find one or two of the activities to be helpful. The following are some general modifications for dramatic play, followed by adaptations that are specific to disabilities.

General Suggestions

▲ Be careful not to make too many rules for the child's play. Enforce only those rules that are really needed for the child to play safely. The child should feel free to experiment and take some risks in play situations (Fisher, Murray, and Bundy 1991).

▲ Reduce distractions when the child is playing.

▲ Include peers in the child's play and teach peers to include the child with special needs.

▲ Instead of giving hand-over-hand assistance to learn play activities, cue peer partners to give play items to the child with special needs and show the child how to use the items appropriately.

▲ Teaching children with special needs to read the social cues of other children is very important.

▲ Let the child take the lead in play. This may involve some patient waiting for the child to choose something to do or careful reading of the child's cues.

▲ Encourage parents to enjoy playing with their child. The parent should not always feel that they must work to improve skills every time they interact with their child.

▲ Some children may need an adult to model play skills.

▲ To encourage children to play together, define the space where children can play and keep it small. For example, position housekeeping toys around a small area rug and remind children that they need to stay on the rug while playing.

▲ Focus play themes on everyday experiences or on play experiences that genuinely seem to interest the child.

▲ Encourage parents to provide dramatic play experiences at home.

▲ Promote communication during play.

▲ Become familiar with the stages of dramatic play. Start with the child's current level of development and encourage the next developmental step.

▲ The housekeeping center is suitable for dramatic play in the classroom. The center should include dress-up clothes, toy plates and utensils, playdough for making food, dolls, doctor kits, strollers, shopping carts, mirror, or props such as a cash register.

▲ Children with attention deficits, autism, and developmental delays tend to flit from center to center. Children cannot fully benefit from the learning experiences in a center if they are there only a moment or two. Insist on children initially spending at least five minutes in a center of their choice and gradually build on the amount of time the child can focus on dramatic play. If five minutes is impossible for the child, start with the amount of time the child can currently tolerate.

▲ To help children put away dramatic play props and toys, label shelves with pictures as well as words (Sheldon 1996).

▲ The more often you interact with children, the less often children interact with their peers. Be careful not to intervene too much in the child's play.

▲ Help the child to develop the language skills she will need to work out conflicts with other children.

Developmental Delays

Adults may be tempted to intervene too much in the play of children with developmental delays. Children need an opportunity to play at their level of ability and to independently initiate play activities. Observing child-initiated play is a good way to evaluate the child's current developmental levels so that you can determine what kind of play experiences would be developmentally appropriate and motivating for the child. If you need to intervene when the child is playing in a group, be as unobtrusive as possible. For example, you could simply sit down as part of the children's play and become a character or prop so that you could subtly make suggestions or cue the children. Always include a peer partner when working on play skills with a child who has developmental delays. The peer partner can model play skills for the child, while you can model how to include both children in play.

▲ The child may have difficulty playing for a long time. Section off an area for play through the use of a refrigerator box or partition. Include another child and an adult in that area. Keep the play at the child's ability level and focused on the child's interest.

▲ Offer dramatic play materials that are familiar and a part of the child's daily life experiences. For example, a pet care center might generate more active play than a spaceship center.

▲ Encourage verbalization during play by asking questions and encouraging communication with other children.

▲ Use picture cues or storybooks to stimulate play and use of language.

▲ Some children with developmental delays fatigue very easily. Make sure that the child has supportive seating.

▲ Teach peer partners how to include children with special needs in their play. Children can be shown how to approach the special needs child, take her hand, and offer a prop. Teach children with special needs key phrases to include themselves in play such as, "What are you doing?" (Monighan-Nourot, Scales, Van Hoorn, and Almy 1987). Sometimes simply joining in is often the best way for the child to enter into a play situation.

▲ The child who is not yet proficient at dramatic play may be able to carry out some kind of support role in the play, such as being the patient at a doctor's office. This can be facilitated by having the appropriate props nearby or by verbally suggesting the role (Monighan-Nourot, Scales, Van Hoorn, and Almy 1987).

▲ Set up a separate play center that is near the other children and includes props that will encourage play. Model how to expand the play. For example, demonstrate how to make noises or sound effects.

▲ Store play props in a box, bringing out a few at a time to avoid unnecessarily distracting the child.

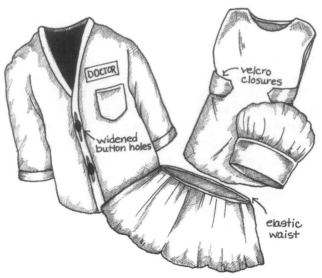

▲ Provide some dress-up clothes that are simple to get on and off and do not have tiny buttons or snaps. Large clothes are easier to get on and off. Make a small snip in the buttonholes of medium to large buttons to make it easier for the child to button and unbutton. Dress-ups can be a fun opportunity to work on dressing skills.

▲ Provide telephones, briefcases, strollers, and other play props that the child sees in her everyday life.

▲ Rather than reading a story to the children to enrich their play, tell them a story. For example, tell a story about children taking care of their pets and bringing them to the veterinarian when the pets are sick (Johnson-Martin, Attermeier, and Hacker 1990).

▲ Making books with photographs of the children in various kinds of play is a powerful tool to teach play skills. The book can be read over and over until the child has learned all the play sequences. Each book should have a separate play theme.

▲ Respond to the child's cues to play, even if they are not age appropriate. Children should be able to be themselves and to play at their current level of development.

Orthopedic Impairments

Correctly positioning this child is essential. She needs to be positioned to maximize functioning while being near peers. Observe the play to ensure that the child is positioned with her body in good alignment and in such a way that she is not totally curled up into flexion or thrown into extension when attempting to move. Consult with the physical or occupational therapist for ideas on positioning. Good positioning will help to reduce drooling, which might increase as the child tries to play. Make sure that the equipment and furniture in the classroom are arranged so that the child can get from one play center to the other independently.

Sometimes, a child comes to school with limited play experience. The child's time may have been taken up with "therapeutic" activities and she may not have had enough access to appropriate toys and opportunities to play independently. The child may also have had many medical procedures or need to take medication that makes her drowsy. The social aspects of play are important for the child with physical disabilities as an opportunity to learn how to interact with other children and to develop language skills. This child will need toys and play props she can successfully manipulate and a communication system that will allow her to interact with the other children if she does not have verbal language. It is very difficult to determine whether or not the young, nonverbal child with orthopedic impairments has cognitive delays. Observing the child's play is one way to investigate the child's developmental levels. Sometimes children with orthopedic problems also have impairments in other areas, such as vision. Make sure that the child's individual needs have been assessed and are addressed in the classroom.

timer

▲ Adapted toys are important for children to develop a sense of cause and effect. Many toys with batteries can be adapted for switches. You must purchase a switch, battery device adapter, and a toy that runs on batteries. A switch latch and timer can also be used to control how long the toy will stay on.

Switch

battery-operated toy

▲ Add weights to equipment, such as wagons and furniture, so that they will not tip if the child leans on them.

▲ Teach the child safety procedures such as beeping the horn on her electric wheelchair before backing up. If the child has crutches or a walker, a place must be designated where the equipment can be left so that no one trips over it.

▲ Provide the child with picture icons to indicate her choice of toys if she does not have functional speech skills. It is very important that children who do not have independent mobility are offered a choice of where they want to play. These children cannot move independently away from play they find boring or toward play that interests them.

▲ Give the child toys that are of interest and easy to manipulate. For example, allow the child to feed a doll with a bottle rather than expecting the child to take off the doll's clothes if the child does not have the necessary fine motor skills. Make sure the child has a wide variety of toys so that she can learn to adapt her movements.

▲ Position the child so that she can be with the other children. For example, if the children are playing on the floor, the child should be out of her wheelchair and in a corner seat.

▲ Observe if the child is always put in a subordinate role of "baby" and intervene to make sure the child has a variety of roles while playing. Props such as a hat and plastic "car keys" could be used for the child to pretend to be the daddy rather than the baby.

▲ Place a small dollhouse, people, and furniture on the child's wheelchair tray to give the child more access to play. Always include another child in the play and vary the play experiences.

▲ Play at the computer can be surprisingly social. If the child has a peer partner nearby, computer programs can offer opportunities for social interaction with one child using the mouse and the other child assisting.

▲ Encourage the children to talk about what they are doing in play using verbal language, or picture symbols and assistive devices such as a SpeakEasy if they do not have verbal language. With the SpeakEasy Voice Output Communication Aid the child is able to press up to twelve icons to trigger a recorded message or word. Please refer to page 190 in the appendix for information on where to order.

Pervasive Developmental Disorder (PDD) and Autism

These children may have self-stimulatory behaviors that get in the way of functional play. Instead of exploring how to use an object, the child may shake or spin it. This child's play may be further compromised by language delays that will impact her ability to play with other children. Sensory defensiveness may make it difficult to tolerate the touch and sound input that comes from active play with other children. If the child does not learn how to play and stays stuck in self-stimulatory behavior, she misses valuable learning experiences about using language functionally, as well as cause and effect and social skills. Some autistic children may learn some basic play skills but not develop imaginative play. Any play skills are important and allow the child to participate in social situations in school and at home. Initially, structure play situations so that the child can be involved in sensory motor play, such as water play while washing a doll, but at the same time be near peers and be part of the symbolic play. Some of the play modifications listed in this chapter for children with developmental delays may also be relevant for children with PDD and autism.

▲ Break down the steps of play to determine where the child is currently functioning and offer play experiences that are developmentally appropriate.

▲ It helps to have two sets of toys so that you can demonstrate appropriate play.

▲ Include motivating objects as part of the play to focus the child's attention on the activity. An example of this approach would be to use train plates or train candleholders if the child is interested in trains to capture her attention during a pretend birthday party activity.

▲ Use picture icons to represent the steps of the play you wish the child to engage in. For example, if you are playing "birthday party," the pictures would show making the cake, putting the candles in, singing, and blowing out candles. Make a book with the icons describing the steps of play or use actual photographs of the children playing.

▲ Reading storybooks with pictures of children approaching and playing with children with special needs may help to reinforce interaction during play time.

▲ Repeat the play experiences for an adequate amount of time for the child to

master all the steps. Our play themes for one year were baby care, pet care, shopping, birthday party, and restaurant. We practiced playing in each theme for one month and then repeated the themes during the second half of the school year. Although this may seem rather tedious, it is important for the child to feel comfortable in a play situation and have a repertoire of things to do that have been adequately practiced. Play skills were initially practiced in the therapy room with the speech and occupational therapist, but were also set up in the classroom for generalization. Parents were encouraged to have the same play props at home. As the child becomes more familiar with the toys and play schemes, more imaginative play sometimes takes place.

▲ The child may actively resist having other children or adults involved in her play. Persist in your efforts; use praise and tangible reinforcement to reward the child's increasing tolerance for playing with others.

▲ Children may want to play with the toys by themselves on the other side of the room. Position the play props and materials on an area rug or mat to establish a play space. Instruct the child that she has to stay on the rug or mat, or that she needs to stay in the "play center." Proximity to other children will facilitate interaction. The child may have an easier time playing near or with other children if the play activity is very interesting.

▲ The child will have an easier time making eye contact if she is not over- or understimulated. See pages 181-184 in the appendix for information on the sensory needs of children.

Attention Deficit Hyperactivity Disorder (ADHD) and Behavioral Issues

Two traits—high activity levels and distractibility—may prevent children from developing play skills. These children are more able to focus on play that they have chosen and that is of personal interest. Novelty is very important. Adding a single novel toy to a play setting may be enough to refocus the child's attention. For example, if the child is playing in the pet care center and seems to be losing interest, add a doctor's kit with stethoscope and play syringe and cue the child to return to the play with a question such as, "Is the dog sick?"

▲ Help children to learn how to work out conflicts when playing with other children. Make sure that all of the children know that you want them to come to you if they need help with another child. The child may need adult help to verbalize what is bothering her rather than acting out aggressively. You can model phrases for the child to use in conflict situations such as, "It's my turn now." Sometimes practicing the social skill is necessary. For example, if the child has difficulty sharing, you might give the child items such as paper tickets to pass out to other children during play. Paper tickets aren't all that desirable, and there are a lot of them, making this a relatively pain-free sharing practice (Allen and Schwartz 1992).

▲ Make sure that there are clear behavioral consequences for inappropriate behavior. Carefully consider whether the rules you make are really necessary.

▲ Watch out for the levels of stimulation in the classroom. Teach all the children in the class that when they hear the phrase "Stop, Look, and Listen" they are to stop what they are doing and look at you. You may have another phrase that you use, but children do need to be cued to attend to you at times when the noise or activity level in the classroom becomes too intense.

▲ Exciting activities that are new or offer a lot of sensory input should be preceded and followed by calming activities. Involvement in dramatic play could be followed by quiet time sitting on a beanbag chair in a small play tent with a favorite toy.

▲ Oral motor toys, such as aquarium tubing for chewing, blow toys, or sour candy, can be calming and organizing for some children. Place these items in a fanny pack and let the child choose an item she feels will help her to relax. See page 189 in the appendix for suggestions.

▲ For other children, the opportunity to move is what is most calming. Allow the child to move before or after activities.

▲ If the child attempts to leave the center after a few moments of play, ask the child to stay and do one more thing (Heidemann and Hewitt 1992). On the other hand children should be allowed to leave play situations that are not productive.

▲ Play that really is of interest to the child may help her to learn to pay attention.

▲ Hyperactivity in and of itself does not get in the way of learning. If the child is focused on the play activity while actively moving about, there is no need to intervene. This differs from the child who cannot focus on the play or the other children, and is darting aimlessly around the classroom. That child needs adult intervention to settle down to play. A weighted vest can be calming for some children.

▲ Reduce distractions in the dramatic play center by hanging sheets or lengths of fabric from the ceiling to section off the center from the rest of the room. The dramatic play could also take place in a large box or under a table that has been draped with a sheet.

▲ Set a timer to help the child stay in a play center. The timer provides an auditory cue for when the child can move to another center and gives the child a sense that her involvement in the center has a definite beginning and end.

Motor Planning Problems

These children would benefit from an opportunity to plan and discuss what they are going to be doing in play. After the child has carried out her plans, give feedback to the child by verbally describing her play or by asking the child to remember and relate what she did in play. The child with motor planning problems typically may struggle with fine motor skills and benefit from adaptations such as Velcro on dress-ups.

▲ Children with motor planning problems should be encouraged to explore the uses of unfamiliar objects and to devise things to do with the objects.

▲ Large, sturdy toys will be easier for the child to manipulate. Small dollhouse furniture or doll clothes might be frustrating for the child with motor planning difficulties.

▲ Some children with motor planning problems will avoid an activity if it looks too challenging. Observe if a child consistently avoids a play center and gently encourage participation by breaking down the activity into manageable steps.

▲ Observe children to determine if the child is getting stuck on one kind of play. The child may be more comfortable with play she has practiced and may need to learn some new play strategies.

▲ Encourage the child to give some of her own ideas for the group to play, rather than always following the other children's plans.

▲ Give lots of praise and warm encouragement to bolster the confidence of children with motor planning difficulties.

Visual Impairments

These children are at risk for difficulties with play because they have not had the opportunity to learn how to play by observing others. The child may also have had limited experience with exploring and manipulating objects. It is important that children with residual vision be encouraged to use their vision. Children who are blind should be encouraged to explore the sensory properties of objects.

▲ Help the child to explore the dramatic play area and to discuss what the objects are and what they are used for. Ask the other children in the center to explain the ongoing play to the child who is visually impaired (Monighan-Nourot, Scales, Van Hoorn, and Almy 1987).

▲ Teach peer partners how to include the child by saying the child's name before speaking (Monighan-Nourot, Scales, Van Hoorn, and Almy 1987).

▲ Ask the child's parents to provide dramatic play props for the child at home so that skills can be practiced and generalized.

▲ Intervene if the child is always assigned subordinate roles in play such as that of the baby or patient and suggest another role.

▲ Encourage the child who is blind to develop social skills that will help her interaction with other children. The child should learn to turn her face toward people when they are talking, to judge how others are reacting from language cues, and to keep her head in midline. Discourage any unusual posturing (Clark and Allen 1985).

Snack Time

7

For some children, snack time is their favorite part of the day; for others, it is a brief distraction from play. Snack time provides a wonderful opportunity for the teacher to help children learn social skills, orgnization skills, self-control, oral motor and fine motor skills. Many children with special needs have oral motor problems. They may be hypersensitive to food textures and tastes. Some children may have low muscle tone in the facial area resulting in an open mouth posture and drooling. With increasing frequency, we see children with complex medical issues, such as gastric tubes, in school settings. Snack can be an important time for introducing a variety of new foods and working on improving oral motor skills.

Social interaction is an important aspect of snack time. While eating with others, a child can practice language skills, such as requesting help from adults or sharing with other children. Sit at the snack table with children to encourage conversation and the use of language when commenting and requesting. This interaction will benefit children with and without special needs. Children can also practice table manners that can be reasonably expected of this age group, such as passing food to another child. Eating slowly without stuffing food into one's mouth is another social skill and a safety issue.

Getting ready for snack, opening the snack, and cleaning up after snack offers opportunities to practice following directions and motor planning. It is important to use the same language every day to help children with language processing problems get through the established routine. Picture icons representing the various steps of the snack routine can be a useful cueing device to help children get ready for snack and clean up afterward. The routine should stress hand washing, getting snack, eating snack, and cleaning up. We recommend that toothbrushing be incorporated as part of the snack routine, not only for dental health, but for the oral motor benefits of decreasing oral sensory defensiveness. Remember to wear gloves during activities such as toothbrushing to protect your health and that of the child. Gloves should be made of vinyl, not latex, because latex can cause an allergic reaction in some children and adults.

The typically developing child attains eating skills in the following sequence. By two years of age, the child is feeding himself and has some control of spoon feeding. The child is able to hold a cup and put the cup down without spilling.

The two-year-old can chew with rotary movements and uses upper and lower lip movements when eating. At three years, the child can feed himself with little spilling. The child handles the spoon efficiently and chews with lips closed. The three-year-old is also able to use a fork to stab food, but prefers to use a spoon. A child between the ages of three to four uses a fork more often and is able to spread with a knife. The child is also able to pour liquids into a glass. The child may eat slowly and be easily distracted by activities or conversation going on around him. Four- to five-year-old children are using the fork, spoon, and knife, although they may need help on occasion. Children this age are able to make some snacks for themselves such as crackers with jelly.

We should let children progress at their own pace in eating. Consistently provide children with the opportunity to experience a variety of foods. Your expectations for snack behavior should be clear to all of the children. It is also very important to work with parents on feeding issues. When the child first enters school, discuss the child's eating habits with parents. Parents tend to send in snack foods they know their child will eat, and you may not be aware that the child is having eating difficulties at home.

Simple cooking activities are important to practice functional fine motor skills, attention to tasks, and following directions. When cooking, children learn to use a knife to spread or a spoon to stir. Hand strength is improved by stirring thick batters or squeezing oranges to make juice. Children learn to follow directions when making simple snacks such as spreading peanut butter on celery and dotting with raisins to make "ants on a log" (Haldy and Haack 1995).

General Suggestions

▲ Expect spilling and messiness when children are learning to eat independently.

▲ When teaching self-feeding skills, break the skills into small sequential steps.

▲ You may need to work with the child's doctor or nutritionist to ensure that the child is receiving adequate nutrition in school and at home. The side effects of some medications can suppress appetite.

▲ All children should be positioned with feet supported and hips flexed when eating.

▲ Snack is such a great opportunity for communication; try to provide the child with alternative communication systems if he does not have verbal language.

▲ Practice other adaptive skills such as hand washing, toothbrushing, cooking, and clean-up during snack time.

▲ A variety of adaptive plates, cups, and utensils can make it easier for the child to be independent in eating.

▲ After the child is eating strained foods, he can progress to mashed or chopped food. Bananas are a good mashed food. The next steps are semisolid food such as cookies crumbled into pudding, followed by solid chewy foods. Cheese or raisins are an example of a solid chewy food. After the child is able to eat these foods comfortably, he can attempt combination foods like soup or difficult chewy solids such as chicken or raw carrots (Evans Morris, and Klein 1987). Make sure to progress at the child's pace when introducing solid foods.

▲ You may want snack to be a center rather than a whole group activity. If a few children are eating at one time, you may find it easier to encourage verbal communication.

▲ Children with special needs have difficulty generalizing skills and will need to practice new eating skills in school and at home. Parents need to be told that school staff cannot establish new eating patterns if these patterns are not carried through at home.

Developmental Delays

The focus of snack for the child with developmental delays should be to increase his independence. The child should be guided into a routine where he gets his own snack, opens up containers whenever possible, and uses utensils effectively.

▲ Establish a consistent routine with clear language. In order to help the child with comprehension problems, use the same verbal cues each day. Varying terms and directions can confuse the child who relies on familiar words.

▲ Utilize "backward chaining" when teaching the child a new skill such as opening a milk carton, eating with a spoon, or toothbrushing. Move the child through the first steps of the task, hand over hand, letting the child do the last step independently. Gradually phase out physical prompts step by step.

▲ The child may not have developed independent eating skills before entering school. The first step toward independence will be mastering eating finger foods. Then the child can move on to using utensils and a cup (Odom and McLean 1996).

▲ To facilitate the learning of routines, identify the child's place and chair with his name and picture. Use placemats stenciled with a place for cup, spoon, and plate.

▲ Use picture icons to portray the steps of the activity and to assist the child in indicating his choice of snacks.

▲ Make sure the child is positioned properly with feet on the floor, sitting upright rather than in a slumped position. Turn the child's chair around so his tummy is against the back of the chair facing the table. This extra support is helpful in keeping the child upright.

▲ Keep an eye on the child while he is eating. A child might quickly stuff his snack into his mouth, which could lead to choking.

▲ Some children need to "wake up" the muscles of the face. Gentle tapping, rubbing, or playing peekaboo may help to improve the child's muscle tone. These games could be paired with a song such as, "This is the way we wake up our face, so early in the morning." Spicy, tart, sour, or cold foods such as popsicles will also facilitate muscle tone.

▲ Quietly cue the child to keep lips closed and wipe chin with a napkin if the child is having difficulty with lip closure when eating.

▲ Learning to use utensils helps to develop hand skills as well as independence in eating. A variety of adapted utensils are available for various problems. For children with poor hand strength, utensils with built-up handles are effective. If the child has difficulty with forearm rotation, spoons and forks that swivel can help compensate for lack of mobility. Weighted utensils help the child with tremors. Bent spoons assist wrist movements for the child who cannot angle the spoon toward his mouth. Child-size utensils can make a big difference for the child with coordination problems. If the child tends to bite the spoon, you can purchase one with a protective Teflon coating.

▲ The child may hold the spoon in a fisted grip initially. Gently cue the child to hold the spoon between thumb and first two fingers. This "tripod" grasp helps to prepare the child's hand for an efficient pencil grip when he is older. If the child does not seem ready for holding the spoon in his fingers, postpone the attempt until he is older. A more mature grip may emerge naturally as the child's hand skills develop.

▲ Playing with small pegs and beads will encourage the development of finger dexterity.

▲ If the child has low muscle tone in the oral motor area with an open mouth posture or drooling, his muscle tone may be improved by giving him thick liquids to drink through a straw or whistles to blow.

▲ In some classrooms, children eat snack when they are hungry, which may result in smaller groups of children eating at one time. This should increase language use by the children, if an adult is positioned at the table to facilitate conversation.

▲ If the child is learning to drink independently from a cup, choose a cup that is easy for the child to manipulate. For some children, this choice will be a cup with two handles; for others, a small cup with no handles might work best. Sippy cups with a top and drinking spout are sometimes helpful as the child transitions from sucking to drinking from a cup. At first, put a small amount of liquid in the cup.

▲ Juice packs can be used to help the child to learn to drink from a straw. When the juice pack is squeezed, the juice is pushed up into the straw where the child can easily suck. Sucking from a straw can help with lip closure and muscle tone in the face.

▲ Children should practice pouring drinks from a pitcher into a cup. Make sure the cup has a wide stable base.

▲ Parents tend to pack finger foods for snack, so you should incorporate some cooking activities at snack time. This will provide the child with a variety of foods to practice eating skills and the use of utensils.

▲ If the child cannot yet communicate with verbal language, he should be provided with picture icons or taught sign language in order to communicate with others.

Orthopedic Impairments

Teachers, therapists, and classroom staff will need to work together as a team to determine the kinds of positioning and equipment that these children will need for snack time. Feel free to ask for help with positioning questions, because they are tricky to figure out and often can be solved by a physical, occupational, or speech therapist who has worked with other children with similar issues.

If the child is eating only pureed food, the educational team should gradually add more solid food to the child's diet. Oral motor development is improved by having foods that encourage chewing. Sometimes, supplementary drinks such as PediaSure are used to give the child extra calories. These drinks can fill the child up, resulting in less interest in food. Discuss with the child's doctor or nutritionist if, during a trial period, the child should take in calories from foods, milk, and juices rather than a drink like PediaSure.

▲ The child's position when eating is crucial for a successful snack time. You must observe the child's trunk, hips, pelvis, head, tummy, arms, and legs to determine if the child is positioned in proper alignment to allow for functional movement. The child's head must be lined up over his shoulders and his chin tucked in slightly to be able to swallow.

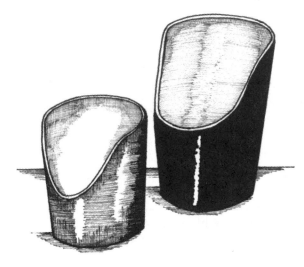

▲ Adaptive cups, dishes, and utensils can significantly improve self-feeding in the child with physical disabilities, if the child is positioned properly for eating. As one of our students with cerebral palsy said, "It's not the spoon, it's my head." She was right! Her shoulders were coming forward, making it difficult to maintain an upright head position and to bring the spoon to her mouth. There are plates and bowls with suction cups on the bottom that provide a stable base. Two-handled cups or cut-out cups make drinking easier. Dycem, a rubberized non-slip material, can also be placed under bowls and cups to decrease sliding and spills. Universal cuffs slip over the child's hand and have a little pocket to hold a spoon or fork for the child with a weak grasp. There are bowls and plates with one side built up to make scooping easier. Please see page 190 in the appendix for information on where to find adapted utensils.

▲ Cups with a cutout for the child's nose can make drinking easier because the child can drink without hyperextending his head.

▲ A spatula spoon with a flat or shallow bowl may be more acceptable for the child with oral hypersensitivities (Odom and McLean 1996).

▲ If the child has a weak grasp, he might benefit from utensils with built-up handles or a Velcro cuff with a pocket for utensils.

▲ Utensils that have a protective coating are helpful for children with a bite reflex.

▲ If the child has a tremor or poor coordination, weighted utensils can be of assistance.

▲ Placing food between upper and lower back teeth stimulates chewing (Odom and McLean 1996).

▲ Explore whether the child is ready to move from adaptive equipment to typical cups, spoons, and utensils. He will be less "separate" when he can use regular utensils.

▲ Some children with physical disabilities need support at their jaw when eating or drinking in order for them to experience a closed mouth position. If you are feeding the child from in front, you would place your thumb under his chin, your middle finger under his jaw, and your index finger along his cheek. If you are positioned to the side of the child, your index finger would go under the child's lip, second finger under the jaw, and thumb along the child's cheek.

▲ Watch that the child does not end up having the same food or consistency of food each day. The child's oral motor skills will not progress if he has yogurt, pudding, or applesauce each day for snack and similar smooth textures for meals at home. After consulting with the child's parents and doctor, introduce various foods, progressing from thick, smooth solids such as pudding to thickened foods such as table foods blended to a thick puree. Eventually you can try mashed solids such as a mashed banana, and later textured early solids. Work with the speech and occupational therapist to move from lumpy to chewy solids. It is essential that the parents also work on a variety of foods at home. If the parents are not ready to vary foods at home, you should consider waiting to work on eating until the parents are ready.

▲ The child should have an opportunity to practice using a spoon and fork as well as eating finger foods.

▲ Fruits and vegetables and extra protein can be hidden in preferred foods. Pureed fruit can be blended with milk or yogurt to make a smoothie that can be sent to school in a thermos. If the classroom has access to a microwave, pureed vegetables can be added to spaghetti sauce at home and the child can have pasta for snack. Macaroni and cheese can be fortified with extra cheese.

▲ Make picture icons so the child can indicate his choice of snack if he does not have functional language.

Snack Time

▲ If the child is medically involved, you may find it helpful to speak to the child's doctor about feeding suggestions. Occasionally, children may have such difficulty swallowing that their liquids need to be thickened to avoid aspiration into the lungs.

▲ Thick-it is a powdered thickener that can be added to any liquid in varying amounts to make a consistency as thick as is needed for the child to swallow. Some children need their liquids thickened to pudding consistency and taken with a spoon.

▲ Involve the child in simple cooking activities as long as they do not increase abnormal movements or muscle tone. For example, the child with spasticity should not stir a resistive batter such as cookie dough that will increase muscle tightness.

Pervasive Developmental Disorder (PDD) and Autism

The challenge for children with PDD and their parents and teachers is to increase the variety of foods the child will eat. These children often overreact to sensory input, including their response to foods. Textured foods often present a problem. The child will clearly prefer familiar to unfamiliar foods in a dramatic way, perhaps eating only four or five foods on a daily basis. Some typically developing children may go through phases where they eat a limited amount of food, but eventually mature and become more willing to eat unfamiliar foods. The child with PDD may not progress to eating a variety of foods without help. Please refer to the orthopedic section for ideas on how to add unfamiliar foods to the child's diet by hiding the new foods in preferred foods.

▲ Slow rocking or swinging before snack and calm music during snack can help the child to be as relaxed as possible.

▲ It has been our experience that sensory integration approaches work well when paired with behavioral interventions. Encouraging tasting of unfamiliar food should be done gently and positively, and be guided by the child's tolerance for the experience. The key is to consistently expose the child to a variety of foods, day after day, at school and at home. Working on eating in a school setting is difficult if the parents are not following through at home. It is also important to break the steps of tasting a new food down into the smallest components. First the child should be expected to just touch the food with a spoon or fork. Once the child has successfully completed the sequence of touching the spoon to the food for three consecutive sessions, move on to the next step. The next step might be scooping a small amount and bringing it toward the lips, but not touching the lips, followed by the step of touching the lips and eventually taking a taste. If the task is broken down into small steps, it is much more comfortable for the child to learn a new skill. Another approach would be to insist on the child's "tasting" a reasonable food such as chocolate pudding if he has only been eating vanilla. It is very important to offer the chocolate pudding for several successive trials to give the child an opportunity to get used to the new taste. If the child has effective chewing and can chew foods such as chips or cookies, he could be offered thin slices of peeled apple or banana instead. A different type of cookie or snack chip might also be a reasonable goal. For children with PDD, behavioral approaches might be necessary to encourage adaptive behaviors, especially if they have not had the experience of trying new foods before entering school and have developed some phobic responses to unfamiliar food. It could take several months of gentle but persistent effort to encourage the child to taste two or three new foods.

▲ The child with tactile hypersensitivities may also benefit from Wilbarger's Deep Pressure Protocol (see page 184 in the appendix for more information). Speak to an occupational therapist to determine if these approaches would be appropriate for the child.

▲ Watch for food allergies in the child who has had a very limited diet when he is exposed to new foods.

▲ It may be possible to mix a new texture or taste with a preferred food. For example, crumble graham crackers into yogurt. Don't change too many variables at once. Alter taste, such as a new flavor yogurt, or temperature, or texture. Don't overwhelm the child by presenting a completely unfamiliar food experience.

▲ Some children with PDD or autism become phobic about foods other than their own "special" foods. Encourage children to handle foods even if they are not going to eat them. For example, the child could be given small amounts of the food that the group will be eating for snack on a plate. If the child only touches the food but will not eat it, he has, at least, interacted with the food. Food preparation and clean-up would be another opportunity for the child to have contact with foods. We have worked with a child who was so anxious about food he would not even pick it up to throw it away. This is a tremendous problem to overcome, and if not addressed during childhood, could seriously impact the child's ability to live independently.

▲ Provide the child with a fanny pack that contains a variety of oral motor toys. You might consider whistles, sour patch candies, nuk brushes, aquarium tubing for chewing, or party blowers. The child should be encouraged to utilize these items to give him oral motor input and decrease tactile defensiveness. See pages 183-184 in the appendix for suggestions.

▲ It is calming for the child with PDD or autism to have predictable routines. Having an assigned chair and snack time routine can help the child to feel more organized at snack time. One program with which we are familiar has the children offer each other choices of snack in a snack bowl. The child verbalizes what he wants, takes a portion of the desired snack, and then passes the bowl onto the next child.

▲ Put a picture icon or photo-graph of snack time on the daily schedule.

▲ Because many children with PDD seem so interested in letters, foods shaped like letters, such as Alphabits cereal, may be good to try.

▲ Make sure that the child's seating is comfortable to encourage staying at the table. The child's feet should reach the ground or be supported by some kind of footstool. Some children may benefit from chairs with arms.

▲ Some autistic children take in a lot of their calories in the form of fluids. Offer fluids after the child has eaten some solid food. Avoid having the child take in lots of calories with liquid supplements such as PediaSure that will make him less interested in food, unless his doctor feels it is necessary.

▲ When introducing toothbrushing, start without toothpaste on the toothbrush. The child may be overwhelmed by the taste of the toothpaste. Parents may have suggestions for toothpaste brands that are acceptable to their child.

▲ Electric toothbrushes can be more acceptable to the child than regular tooth-brushes.

Attention Deficit Hyperactivity Disorder (ADHD) and Behavioral Issues

Typical problem behaviors at snack time include children getting up and run-ning around the classroom before they have eaten their snack, children eating someone else's snack, and difficulty with communicating needs verbally.

▲ Helping the child to stay seated long enough to eat is a key issue for chil-dren with ADHD. Given clear expectations and firm limits, the child can gradual-ly lengthen his tolerance for sitting, although adults must realize that the child's nervous system makes this a very difficult chore.

▲ If the child eats too quickly, give him small amounts of food. Part of a cookie, a few pieces of cereal, or crackers will help the child to learn to chew and swallow before taking another bite. This practice may help the child to avoid choking.

▲ Some children are extremely distractible and may need a very quiet environ-

ment to be able to focus on eating. Eating in a quiet, non-distracting part of the classroom with one or two other children may be necessary for the child to finish snack.

▲ Be aware that the child with ADHD may have some sensory defensiveness in response to various textures or tastes. Work with parents to gradually increase the variety of foods.

▲ Avoid power struggles with these children over food. Do not attempt to trick the child into trying new foods. Simply offer appropriate foods during snack time, then remove them when snack is over. If the child's food avoidance is severe, long-standing, and affects his nutrition, you may want to try some of the gradual food introduction suggestions detailed in the PDD and Autism section on pages 122-123.

▲ Consider the timing of medication in whether or not the child will be interested in eating snack. Ritalin can cause nausea, stomach pain, decreased weight, and decreased appetite.

▲ A timer may help the child stay at the snack table for a reasonable amount of time.

Motor Planning Problems

These children have poor coordination when opening containers or using utensils. The child may also have poor sensory awareness and not notice if food or drink is on his face or chin.

▲ Children with motor planning difficulties may initially need hand-over-hand instruction to learn to effectively use utensils. Phase out physical assistance as the child learns this skill.

▲ This is a child who might do well with a sippy cup or another type of cup with a top to prevent frequent spills.

▲ The child may have motor planning difficulties in the oral motor area that result in problems with chewing and efficiently moving food around in the mouth. These skills can be strengthened with specific exercises. Encourage the child to imitate facial movements in a mirror such as smiles, frowns, tongue waggling, kisses, or surprised looks.

▲ Teach the child to check in a mirror after snack to make sure his face is clean.

▲ Use non-breakable pitchers, cups, and plates for drinking and pouring. Weighted utensils may give the child more sensory feedback and improve coordination.

▲ The child with motor planning problems may be a messy eater. Positioning a tabletop mirror in front of the child while he is eating will give visual feedback to wipe his face. Other children at the table may enjoy watching themselves eat snack.

▲ Teach the child to spread peanut butter or jelly on crackers or other simple cooking activities by breaking the task into small steps. Use photographs or line drawings to illustrate the steps of the cooking activity.

▲ Make sure this child is positioned with feet firmly on the floor or a supporting surface, with hips back in the chair, and head and back in alignment.

Visual Impairments

Suzanne Evans Morris and Marsha Dunn Klein in their book, *Pre-feeding Skills*, have effective suggestions for feeding the child with visual impairments. Establishing familiar routines will help to teach children how to eat independently. The more children are able to do on their own, the more confident they will be in their ability to learn new skills and grow.

▲ Set up the child's snack in a familiar pattern to encourage independence. Encourage the child to use his hands to explore the area, locating plates, cups, and utensils. Use a tray or placemat to define the eating space. The child should learn to replace items in their routine position, so he can find them again.

▲ If the child needs hand-over-hand assistance with utensils, cue the child that food is coming with a verbal prompt or by toucing the child's lip with a spoon.

▲ Morris and Klein suggest that the teacher be sensitive to the child's food preferences and the timing of when the child wishes the next bite. Encourage the child to do as much as possible for himself by gradually phasing out adult assistance.

Transitions

8

Transition times occur when children move from one activity to another. Arriving at school and leaving school are transition times. Going to the bathroom is a transition, and so is going from circle time to the art center. Most transitions occur in group situations, such as moving from a large group into a small group. Most teachers try to engage children in activities throughout the day, yet in many school settings young children are pulled out of their play to transition to another activity and are expected to wait idly for extended periods of time. Current appropriate practice does not support idle waiting during transition times. These times are, instead, viewed as an opportunity to engage in activity.

General guidelines for facilitating smooth transitions include dividing children into smaller groups, sticking to daily routines, and giving ample warning prior to transition time. Jean Feldman's *Transition Time: Let's Do Something Different* and J. Grace's *Preschool Games: Terrific Transitional Activities for Your Preschool Classroom* are two books that provide a variety of ideas for making transitions into meaningful experiences. Sing a song, count, imitate hand movements or facial expressions, or use alternate ways to move from one place to another. Transitions also provide a great opportunity to work on language skills. Ask open-ended questions about children's play plans, the day, or any other topic.

Developmental Delays

Children with developmental delays need a longer time to move through transitions, extra cues, and assistance. These children might need to play a few extra minutes before clean-up, watch what the other children are doing first, or wait for a suggestion from the teacher. Sometimes, you just need to provide a simple verbal reminder: "Michael, please help Lisa put the blocks in the basket." This example of cueing the child with specific, concrete words is preferable to the more general cue, "It's clean-up time." Some children with moderate or severe delays also benefit from teacher modeling and direct instruction.

When a young child with developmental delays is new to a school or program, give her extra days or even weeks to explore the room and toys before expecting her to comply to routines and changing activities. Even when the child begins to understand the daily schedule, we still might see inconsistent behaviors. Some days, the child will feel truly integrated, adjusting well to the flow of the activities and functioning fairly independently. On other days, the child may seem to have taken ten giant steps backward. For instance, let's take a child who normally is able to put her jacket on independently and is suddenly unable to do so. Maybe the commotion of many children dressing for an outdoor activity is confusing and distracting, or maybe some small detail in the daily routine

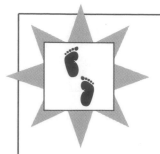

has changed and completely thrown the child off. Whatever the reason, this child will require varying amounts of assistance from day to day to make it through transitions and self-help activities. The following transition modifications are written for children with developmental delays in mind, but are also appropriate for children with PDD, autism, ADHD, or behavioral issues.

▲ Try to perform dressing and undressing activities in the same order each time. Provide a running verbal account of what the child is doing while she is doing it. "Jessica is taking her mittens off first...good job taking your mittens off...then Jessica takes her hat off...good job taking your hat off."

▲ Use the technique of backward chaining to help the child learn to dress and undress independently. In backward chaining, the entire task is completed for the child with the exception of the last step. Work the child on mastering the last step of the process. Once the child is able to do the last step independently, then let the child tackle the next to last step. Continue this backward chaining until the child is able to complete all the steps of the dressing task independently.

▲ For the child with limited language skills, putting on outdoor clothing might signal the time to go home instead of time for outdoor play, or vice versa. Use picture cues to help the child understand the nature of the transition. For instance, a picture of a school bus or a mini-van means time to go home while a picture of the playground or a piece of outdoor playground equipment means it is time to go outside to play.

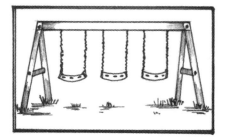

▲ Use clothing that is easy to get on and off: pants with elasticized waists, jackets without elasticized waists, Velcro closures instead of snaps or buttons. In general, large, loose clothing that is one or two sizes too big is easier for children to handle.

▲ There are simple ways to modify clothing that might make dressing and undressing easier. One way is to sew a few short strips of Velcro to the jacket opening to eliminate zipper and button challenges. If you feel the child is ready to learn how to button, make buttonholes larger by snipping the ends of the hole and restitching. For children with muscle weakness or low muscle tone, attach a shower curtain ring to the zipper pull so that the child can use her whole hand to pull the zipper up or down.

▲ Here are some tricks for teaching a child how to get a jacket on independently: (1) Place the open jacket on the floor or table with the collar end of the jacket next to the child. Show the child how to slide her arms into the sleeves and then flip the jacket over her head. (2) Leave the jacket zipped up part way so that the child can step into the jacket. (3) Hang the jacket from a clothesline with two clothespins. Have child back into the jacket and place arms in sleeves.

Then as she walks forward, she will pull the jacket off the line. (4) Place the open jacket on a child's chair and have the child sit on the chair. Prompt the child to place one arm into a sleeve, assisting as necessary. Repeat for the other arm.

▲ Make arrival time into a routine, just as other parts of the day might be. Greeting each child with a daily song or rhyme might be one way to do that. The song/rhyme could incorporate some of the transition tasks that the child needs to do before she can go play. For instance, sing the following to the tune of "Farmer in the Dell": "Good morning, Michael. Good morning, Michael. It's so nice to see you, come in to your school. Please hang your things up. Please hang your things up. Then choose a center tag and play for a while."

▲ If feasible, have the same adult greet the children each morning and the same adult send off the children in the afternoon. Consistency is important for building a sense of confidence and control.

▲ To help children stay in line when walking from one location to another, have them hold onto a rope that has been marked with strips of colored tape at two-foot (sixty-centimeter) intervals.

▲ Post a pictorial representation of the day's schedule in the room. You can refer to this schedule throughout the day as the children move from one activity to another.

▲ Hang the child's name sign or photograph in the center that she is going to next.

Orthopedic Impairments

The child with orthopedic impairments frequently requires assistance to move from place to place. This assistance might be physical help from an adult or another child to push a wheelchair or open a door, to transfer the child from the chair to the floor, or to provide the child with the appropriate adaptive equipment. One of the biggest challenges for the child with orthopedic impairments during transition times is being able to get from one place to the next in the same amount of time as the child's able-bodied peers. Frequently, for the sake of expediency, teachers end up doing things for the child that the child could actually do for herself if given sufficient time. This situation poses a conflict for the teacher who wants to promote independence, but knows that in doing so, the child will need much more time to complete the same tasks than the other children. Is it better to let the other children wait while the child with orthopedic impairments dresses herself or should you offer assistance in the interest of the other children in your room? We hope that some of the suggestions listed below will help the child with orthopedic impairments function as independently as possible within the context of the time constraints of a typical school day.

▲ Let the child use a coat hook and cubby that are located at one end of the row of cubbies, rather than in the middle. This location gives the child more space without getting in the way of other children who are also at their cubbies.

▲ Make the coat hook and cubby accessible from a wheelchair. This might mean moving the coat hook and/or cubby up or down to an appropriate height for the child.

▲ Always have the child place an affected arm into the sleeve first when putting on a jacket or sweater. When removing a jacket, always remove an affected arm first. Some of the dressing techniques described in the section on developmental delays might be appropriate for the child with orthopedic impairments, but you might want to consult with an occupational therapist for more specific suggestions.

▲ Some children with mild orthopedic impairments prefer sitting on the floor or on a child-size chair for dressing tasks. Other children benefit from additional support in the form of a beanbag chair, a corner seat, or cushions placed around the back and sides.

▲ A child in a wheelchair can feel useful when asked to hold the door open for the other children during a transition time. Transition times are perfect for finding jobs for the child with orthopedic impairments. Because these children frequently take longer to get from one place to another, let this child go ahead a few minutes early to assume her job position.

▲ Set up the room so that all centers are easily accessible. You might need to rearrange furniture so that a child with a wheelchair, walker, or crutches can move about freely. Also check rugs and carpets for curled or raised edges or slippery bottoms and tape them down to the floor if necessary.

▲ Consider doing transitions in small groups rather than as one large group. For instance, if children have to leave the room in order to use the bathroom, the child with orthopedic impairments might be able to leave with one group, but return with another group, giving the child extra time to complete toileting skills independently.

▲ Because some children with orthopedic impairments can't move out of play centers independently, they end up staying in only one center, even though they are actually finished playing. Give the child frequent choices so she can let you know when she is ready to transition to another center, or provide her with some way of communicating to you that she needs assistance to move to her next play area. For instance, place a small bell on the child's wheelchair tray or let the child use an augmentative communication device. See catalogs listed on page 190 in the appendix for more information.

▲ Let other children assist the child with orthopedic impairments through transitions. Of course, close adult supervision will be necessary, but transitions offer children with different ability levels a perfect opportunity to interact within the context of a functional activity.

Pervasive Developmental Disorder (PDD) and Autism

Children with PDD and autism frequently get stuck doing inappropriate repetitive activities until someone transitions them to a different activity. This type of behavior, which includes spinning wheels, exaggerated rocking, hand flapping, and other visually stimulating activities, requires that you actively help these children transition not only through the daily routine, but continually throughout the day from their preferred isolating behaviors to more functional play situations. Many children with PDD and autism receive specialized instruction from a trained professional in school and often at home as well. A number of different approaches are currently being used in working with young children who have a diagnosis of PDD and autism. All the professionals and parents should coordinate their approaches to provide as much consistency as possible on a daily basis. Current data indicates that between seventy-five and eighty percent of children with PDD or autism are mentally retarded. Check the section on developmental delays for additional ideas on how to modify transition times for these children.

▲ Provide a photo or pictorial representation of the day's schedule. Present and discuss the day's schedule during morning circle time.

▲ Place the daily schedule pictures on cards that can be removed from a sleeve so that you and the child can fetch the appropriate card prior to each transition to reinforce that it is almost time to change activities.

▲ Try to do the dressing and undressing routine in the same order each time, for example, mittens first, then hat, then jacket. Praise the child for whatever assistance she gives you during the activity, no matter how insignificant it seems to you. "You held out your hand so I could take your mitten off. Thank you."

▲ Reinforce the sameness of the dressing routine by using picture cue cards, line drawings or photographs that show each step of the process. Black and white line drawings work better than photographs.

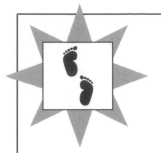

▲ Many children with PDD, autism, or developmental delays who have limited language skills have difficulty understanding why they are putting on their outdoor clothing. Is it time to go home or time to play outside? For these children, a picture cue might help communicate the reason for getting into their jackets. For instance, a picture of a school bus or a mini-van could indicate that it is time to go home, while a picture of the playground or a piece of outdoor playground equipment could indicate that it is time to go outside to play.

▲ Use the same words or simple phrases each time to cue the child about the particular transition. Examples are "circle time is all done," "time to eat snack," "let's go outside," and "put your coat here." Stoop down so that you are at the child's eye level when speaking to him.

▲ Use songs to cue the child as to what activity is coming next. Make up your own songs or look at the activity idea books on transitions that are listed in the introduction to this chapter on page 127.

▲ The child with PDD or autism may not respond to the typical clean-up song or other cues that many schools use. You can go over to where the child is playing and continue to sing the clean-up song in a soft voice or a whisper as you put the toys away. As you model the expected behavior, exaggerate the dropping of each item into the basket or bin by releasing each toy deliberately a few inches above the surface of the container. Some children may need hand-over-hand assistance when learning to pick up.

▲ Mechanical things such as light switches fascinate some children with PDD or autism. You can make this interest more functional by letting the child flash the lights to let the other children know that it is transition time.

▲ If the child with PDD exhibits behaviors that include jumping, then use jumping as a means of locomotion from one activity to another for the entire group. This is another example of how you might take an existing behavior and incorporate it into the classroom routine, making it functional.

▲ For some children who relate well to letters and numbers even at very young ages, you can assign numbers or words to each part of the daily schedule. Put this information on paper so the child has a visual picture of the daily routine to help her understand what is happening when the children leave one activity and go to the next.

▲ Use slow, rhythmic music to help the child calm down for rest time. Music without words (instrumentals) seems to work better than music with singing.

▲ Provide opportunities for other calming sensory input. Examples include: lying under a pile of soft cushions, wrapping up tightly in a blanket, lying inside a mummy-shaped sleeping bag, and wearing a weighted vest or a heavy backpack. Remember to alter the weight in the vest or backpack after 10-15 minutes or remove it entirely after about 20 minutes.

▲ If the child has difficulty letting go of one activity and moving on to the next, let the child take an item from the center that she is playing in to reassure her that she can return to that center later in the day.

▲ An alternative to the above suggestion is to bring the child an object from the next activity center. For instance, if the child is balking at transitioning from blocks to housekeeping, get a toy from the housekeeping center for the child to hold.

▲ Some children will still need physical assistance to transition from one activity to the next, even with the implementation of the above modifications. Providing the child with a tangible reinforcer such as food or a preferred toy might be motivating, but you need to discuss this approach with the child's parents and the other professionals who work with the child.

Attention Deficit/Hyperactivity Disorder (ADHD) and Behavioral Issues

Children with ADHD and behavioral issues thrive on routine and structure. Some children with behavioral problems come from chaotic and disorganized home environments where they don't know what to expect from one minute to the next, so it is especially important for the school or childcare setting to provide them with a predictable routine. Although on any given day a child might have difficulty moving out of one particular activity and into another, transitions that are carried out in a smooth, consistent manner can actually help children feel secure and make sense of their day.

▲ Children should know what to expect—what happens first, next, etc. Reinforce the routine throughout the day by reminding the children of the schedule, posting a picture story of the day's events, and spending a few minutes quietly orienting the child to the school day when she first arrives.

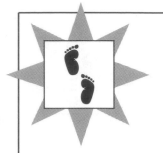

▲ Some children need to sit quietly with an adult for a few minutes when they arrive at school. By the time they get to school, they have already transitioned twice—once from home to the bus or car, and again from the bus or car to the classroom. Also, the morning at home is usually a scene of multiple transitions—getting out of bed, toileting, eating, and dressing are all done under the pressure of the clock. By the time the child arrives at school, she is already stressed from a morning of meeting deadlines.

▲ Some children prefer using their arrival time for running and jumping—a time to "shake the ants out of their pants." You might want to consider using arrival time as outdoor time or gym time instead of indoor playtime. Or perhaps you have enough adults to give children a choice between a quiet arrival time and a more active one.

▲ One way to avoid typical transition problems such as pushing or hitting is to reduce waiting time. Plan transitions so that small groups can move from one place to the next without undo waiting.

▲ Try to incorporate an activity during transitions such as singing a song, imitating movements or facial expressions, or pretending to be a robot or an elephant. More ideas can be found in Jean Feldman's *Transition Time: Let's Do Something Different* or J. Grace's *Preschool Games: Terrific Transitional Activities for Your Preschool Classroom.*

▲ If the child is engaged in a particular activity and is having difficulty letting go to move on to the next, let the child take an item from the previous activity to help reassure her that she can return to that center at a later time.

▲ About ten minutes ahead of time, remind the child that the activity is about to end, and repeat the reminders several times during the course of the next ten minutes.

▲ Try to coordinate the approach you use for transitions with the approach that the parents are using at home. Talk to the parents about what works and what doesn't to come up with a mutually agreeable system.

▲ Bring the children back to the circle time or rug area between activities. Let them sit and regroup for about fifteen seconds before going on to their next activity.

▲ Try to always have the next activity ready in order to reduce waiting time. Excessive waiting is frequently the time that many children become restless and aggressive.

▲ Young children can't easily interpret whether another child has intentionally or accidentally touched or bumped into them. Frequently, the child's response is to hit back. Make sure that there is sufficient space between children during transition times. Transition in small groups, space children in lines along markers on the floor or holding onto tape markers on a rope, and try to reduce waiting time as much as possible.

▲ Because many of these children have difficulty sticking with one activity, they may be only too willing to transition. Use a timer to indicate the end of the activity. Set the timer for a reasonable length of time so that the child can play successfully.

Motor Planning Problems

Most transitions involve putting toys away (clean-up time) and moving to a different part of the room to begin another activity. Children with motor planning problems might not have many difficulties with transition times because the physical challenges are usually minimal and there are frequent opportunities to practice during the course of the day. Because transitions are usually done in groups, the child can observe what other children are doing first and then imitate their motions. The transition times that are probably the most difficult for the child with motor planning issues are dressing and undressing. Many of the dressing suggestions listed on pages 127-129 in the section on children with developmental delays are also appropriate for the child with motor planning problems.

▲ Encourage children to verbalize where they are going when transitioning from one center to the next. Talking about the sequence of the activity beforehand sometimes helps the child with motor planning issues to form a mental image of how her body needs to move in order to get to the next activity.

▲ Make sure that traffic paths are cleared of clutter so that the child doesn't have to negotiate around extraneous obstacles.

▲ Give the child something heavy to put away before transitioning. This type of activity provides the child with sensory input to the muscles and joints which helps her organize and plan her movements.

▲ Once a child arrives in the next center, encourage the child to verbally describe her plan of action: what is she going to do and how is she going to do it. Verbalizing helps the child organize and plan. Also use this intervention during dressing and undressing activities.

▲ In addition to verbalizing a plan of action, you can draw stick figure pictures of the child's plan of action as she describes them. The pictures might help the child form a mental image of the activity to which she can refer the next time.

▲ Simplify dressing tasks by doing the steps in the same order each time. Use backward chaining.

Visual Impairments

The child with visual impairments might need more time than other children to become accustomed to a new school setting and all its transitions. This child might prefer to spend days or even weeks in one play area rather than joining the larger group for activities and transitions in order to gather auditory information about the flow of the day and the scope of activities. Allow the visually impaired child this opportunity to become more secure in her new environment before expecting the child to participate in all the day's transitions.

▲ Assign the child a coat hook and cubby at the beginning or end of the row and place a tactile cue just below it. Use this same cue when you need to identify other items that belong to the child such as a mat or chair. Examples of tactile cues include a strip of sandpaper, Velcro, or satin cloth.

▲ Instead of a tactile marker for the cubby area, use an auditory marker such as a small bell. Hang the bell just above the child's coat hook.

▲ Give the child verbal information about the location of items in the room. Is the sand table next to the window or the cubbies? Here are the shelves for the blocks. What will you find when you walk around to the other side of the shelves?

▲ Use the rug area as a sort of home base during transitions. Make it the place the children always return to after each activity and from which they set out to find the next activity. This can be a good way to introduce the child to the physical layout of the room because you are giving the child a reference point; everything in the room can be located in reference to the rug area.

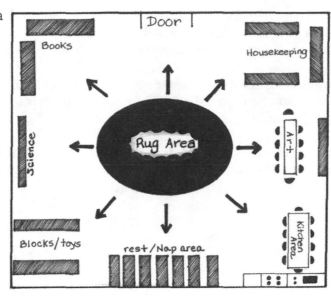

▲ Sometimes the child appears to be wandering aimlessly around the room during center time. Don't be too quick to intervene because this child might actually be exploring her options by carefully gathering information from the auditory cues around her.

▲ Transition time can be utilized as an opportunity to reinforce social skills, especially sharing and asking for help. The child might need assistance with dressing when arriving at school or when getting ready to leave. You might model how to ask another child or adult for help, or actually instruct the child on how to recognize when she needs help and then how to request that help.

▲ Define the areas of the room by using different floor coverings or boundary markers: indoor-outdoor carpeting for the block center, a different texture rug for the circle area, and masking tape to indicate the boundary of the art area.

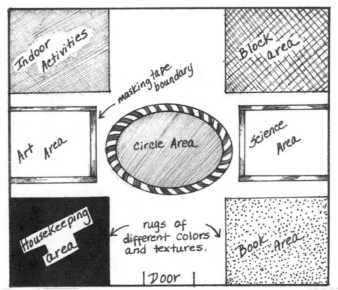

▲ Another way to define the areas of the room is to paint the edges of bookshelves, tables, and door frames with a contrasting color or line with colored tape.

▲ Glue or staple Velcro strips to the walls and furniture to use as a guide when traveling around the room.

Transitions

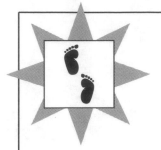

▲ Allow extra time for the child to complete transitions. If you need to offer the child physical assistance, walk in front or next to the child. You do not have to hold onto the child, but allow the child to hold your hand or arm.

▲ Make the room safe for the child with visual impairments by padding sharp corners on furniture with a thick layer of fabric or batting and removing clutter. Try to maintain a simple, organized room.

▲ Use consistent auditory cues to indicate transition time. For instance, ring a bell for a five-minute warning, then follow with a consistent song or rhyme.

The Inclusive Classroom

Fine Motor Center

9

For the school-age child, fine motor skills are usually associated with how well the child writes, colors, and cuts. For the preschool child, fine motor skills are those skills that prepare children for school-age activities. At the preschool level we encourage children to do lots of paper tearing; play with clay; handle small items such as beads, beans, and pennies; and practice two-handed activities such as screwing nuts and bolts together and opening containers. Fine motor activities include functional tasks such as closing zip-closure bags, picking up pennies and other coins, using tongs to pick up objects, spraying bottles for cleaning, folding laundry such as facecloths, and hanging clothes with clothespins.

You might come across occupational therapists or other professionals who talk about fine motor skills in terms of grasp, release, hand and finger strength, eye-hand coordination, bilateral coordination (using two hands together), and the development of a dominant hand. Although these terms are helpful when describing a child's fine motor ability and for developing a clinical therapy program, you should consider any fine motor activity in your classroom as an opportunity for children to practice all the aspects of fine motor skill development.

The development of a dominant hand is frequently a subject of concern for parents and teachers. Genetics and the maturity of the child's nervous system influence hand dominance. Although some children begin to indicate a preferred hand at a very young age of one or two, many children need years of practicing with both hands together before settling on a dominant hand. Even once a child has "decided" to use his left hand for coloring and writing, for instance, he might feel more comfortable using his right hand for cutting. This type of hand-specific skill development is quite common, especially for children whom we might label left-handed. Current research indicates that many children continue to develop hand dominance until about the age of seven, so don't spend too much time fretting over this issue with younger children. Simply continue to provide plenty of opportunities for using both hands together and the rest should take care of itself in time.

Fine motor skills develop after the child has a good foundation in large muscle skills and continues to improve with regular practice. We cannot emphasize enough the importance of developing the large muscles and corresponding joint stability for the successful development of more refined skills such as writing and coloring, buttoning, handling small objects for gluing projects, and using paper clips. If a child's trunk is weak and the muscles around the shoulder do not stabilize the shoulder joint sufficiently, the child's arm consequently moves around too freely, sort of like a Raggedy Ann doll. When this happens, the hand

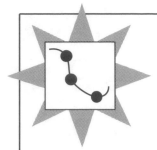

and fingers do not have a stable base from which to work and the result is immature or awkward grasp patterns, tremulous movements, and poorly coordinated release patterns.

You can think about poor joint stability in terms of a roller that is used to paint walls. Imagine using such a roller if the cylinder part of the tool were dangling from the handle instead of being firmly secured. You probably would not have much control over the movement of the roller and would soon become frustrated. Of course, you have the luxury of going to the store to replace that dysfunctional tool, but a child with poor joint control must find ways to compensate or face the prospect of failure. Some of the suggestions that we list in the following sections offer those children with weak or immature muscle development alternative ways to work with beads, blocks, pegs, and other manipulatives. We also want to encourage you to provide activities that will help children continue to develop the large muscles and joint stability necessary for playing with manipulatives. These activities include digging, push and pull games (wagons, wheelbarrows, push toys, shovels and other digging tools), playing on hands and knees, and carrying heavy objects.

Unfortunately, the children you would most like to have practice fine motor skills are usually the ones who avoid these activities. These children have probably attempted manipulative activities, but have found them difficult or frustrating. Some children might become anxious about their experiences with manipulatives, while others give up. Children with tactile defensiveness may have difficulty tolerating hand-over-hand assistance while manipulating objects that they find unpleasant to touch. In this chapter, we will provide you with some suggestions to help all children, including those who might have tactile defensiveness, participate in the fine motor center.

Following the typical development of fine motor skills in young children, we would expect two-year-olds to imitate circular scribbles and vertical and horizontal strokes while holding crayons in a fist. The two-year-old will also place rings onto a stick and put large pegs into a pegboard. Between the ages of two to three years, the child learns to string beads, turn the pages of a book, snip with scissors, and place simple shapes into a form board. At this age the child also begins to hold crayons with the thumb and fingers rather than the fist and begins to use one hand consistently in activities. By the time a child reaches the age of four, he is able to build a tower of nine blocks, drive nails and pegs with a hammer, copy a circle, and imitate a cross. The child's crayon grasp has usually matured to a three- or four-finger grasp, although much of the crayon movement still originates in the action of the wrist and forearm. The four-year-old child can also assemble a puzzle with seven to fifteen pieces. The five-year-old child uses scissors to cut on a line continuously, copies a cross and a square on paper, and prints a few capital letters. Five-year-olds and children older than five rely less on the movement of the wrist and forearm for coloring and are beginning to use efficient finger movements to control a crayon on paper.

We have talked about the fine motor center in terms of motor skill development. However, manipulatives should also be used as an integral part of developing

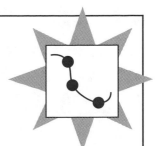

thinking skills and concept formation. Sorting, matching, and memory games can be incorporated into your manipulative center using the modifications that we present in this chapter.

General Suggestions

▲ Self-help skills are great for working on fine motor strength and dexterity. Encourage children to use buttons, zippers, and snaps, giving them only as much assistance as they need.

▲ Encourage parents to involve children in household chores such as ripping up junk mail, folding facecloths, or picking up toys.

▲ Make sure the activities are of interest to the child to capture the child's attention. Include some of the following in your fine motor centers: paper of various thicknesses for snipping; snaps, buttons, and zippers; geoboards, hammering sets, pop beads and other interlocking toys; Bristle Blocks, shape boxes, wooden blocks of various sizes, Legos, Tinkertoys, snap blocks; wooden beads and strings, lacing, stringing for necklaces; hair rollers, buttons, straws, thread spools, toilet paper rolls, paper clips, and Lifesavers for stringing; puzzles, nesting cups; pegs and peg boards, Mr. Potato Head, Lite Brite, Bedbugs; tops, wind-up toys; clothespins, rolling pins, tweezers, tongs; small items for pushing through slits made in the plastic lids of containers; dolls for dressing and undressing; doll clothes for washing and hanging on a line to dry; stickers; toy hammers; seeds for planting; chalk for writing on sidewalk, ink for stamping activities.

▲ Many children need a non-distracting setting when learning new fine motor skills. Block distractions with partitions, by hanging fabric from the ceiling, or by placing bookcases on the tabletop. Commercial tabletop dividers can also be purchased.

Developmental Delays

Children with developmental delays frequently need a bit more structure and guidance than typically developing children when using small manipulatives. A three-year-old who is functioning at the two-year level in most areas of performance will find many of the typical preschool fine motor activities frustrating or uninteresting. Although this child is not able to string beads, he might think that pushing the beads through a hole in the top of a container is lots of fun. Modifying an activity to fit the developmental level of the child will help the child play for longer periods of time, and feel successful and confident.

The manipulative center might also pose a potential safety and health risk for the child with developmental delays. Mouthing objects is how some children who are developmentally delayed explore the environment. Items on the fine

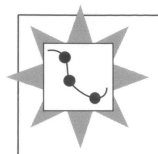

motor table might be small enough to swallow or lodge in a child's throat, so these children must be supervised closely. Throwing objects is another common behavior of some children with developmental delays. Although careful monitoring is recommended, we again encourage you to modify the materials and activities to the child's ability level in order to help reduce inappropriate or dangerous behaviors.

Some children with developmental delays have problems with overall muscle development in both the large and small muscles of the body, resulting in poor fine motor skills. These children might also have short attention spans and difficulty focusing on tasks. You might find that some of the suggestions in other sections of this chapter, especially those devoted to children with orthopedic impairments (pages 145-146), PDD/autism (pages 147-148), and ADHD/behavioral issues (pages 148-150) might also work for children with developmental delays.

▲ Observe children to determine what kind of fine motor activities and manipulatives interest them. This is a great way to assess the child's level of skill and to determine which activities will be interesting and motivating.

▲ Although it is tempting to give the child larger manipulatives such as large Duplo blocks or beads, smaller manipulatives actually encourage more finger dexterity. Start the child out with items that are easy to manipulate, but move as quickly as possible to smaller objects that require children to use their fingers rather than relying on gross grasp patterns.

▲ Offer hand-over-hand assistance as necessary for new activities. Accompany the physical assistance with simple verbal cues. Gradually phase out the physical assistance and just use the verbal cues.

▲ Use pipe cleaners instead of string to teach stringing beads. You can also dip string in glue and let it dry to create a stiff threading device similar to a pipe cleaner. These firm threading devices are much easier to handle than flimsy string.

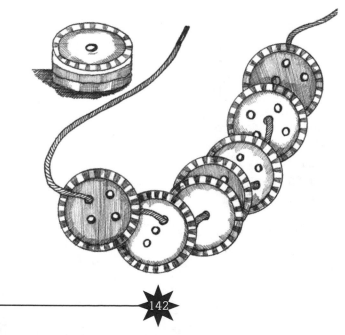

▲ String metal, rubber, or plastic washers instead of beads. Choose beads that are squat instead of long so that the string comes through the other side of the hole without excessive manipulation.

▲ If stringing beads is too difficult, try an alternative activity placing metal, plastic, or rubber washers onto thin dowels. Stick the dowels into a clay or Styrofoam base for support or wrap a thick coating of masking tape or elastic band around one end of the dowel to prevent the washers from slipping off.

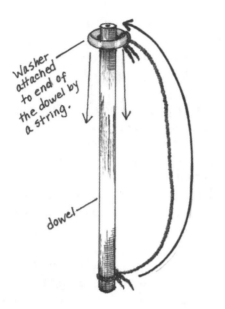

Washer attached to end of the dowel by a string.

dowel

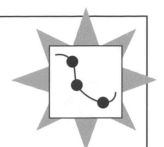

▲ For children who insist on throwing things on the floor, tie one washer or large bead onto a string that has been secured to the bottom of the dowel. Make sure the string is long enough so the washer can reach the top of the dowel. You can add a few more washer-string combinations after the child has mastered the first one.

▲ Jumbo pegs are usually easier for a young child with unskilled hands or low muscle tone to manipulate. Commercial sets are available in specialty stores and catalogs or you can make your own by using empty film containers as pegs and an inverted egg carton with holes cut into the bottom for the pegboard. Fill the film canisters with sand to make them heavier and provide more sensory feedback.

▲ Place the entire fine motor activity into a cookie sheet or other shallow container to help focus the child's attention on the activity. This type of intervention also helps define the child's play space.

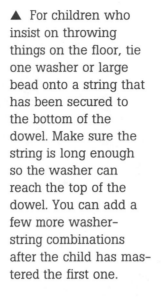

Cut holes in bottom of egg carton.

use empty film canisters for "pegs".

▲ Modify peg or bead activities so that they meet the developmental needs of the child. For instance, you might cut a hole in the top of an empty coffee can and let the child drop the beads, pegs, metal washers, or bottle caps into the container. The sound of the beads or washers hitting the bottom of the metal container provides immediate positive feedback. If you need to make this activity more challenging, cut holes or slits that are either the same diameter as the peg or bead or even a tiny bit smaller. The child will then have to push each manipulative piece through the opening instead of simply dropping it.

▲ Children with developmental delays frequently enjoy activities that are repetitive. Model ways to interact with playdough or clay that lend themselves to repetition. Hammer the playdough, pull off small pieces of playdough to place on top of golf tees that have been pushed into a Styrofoam base, push golf tees or another manipulative into a long playdough snake, or drive a small car across an expanse of flattened playdough.

▲ Make available developmentally appropriate manipulatives such as large pop beads, a ring stack, simple nesting cups, and a variety of containers to fill and empty.

▲ Manipulatives that offer some resistance are great for building up the muscles of the hand. Resistive toys include snap blocks, pop beads, Bristle Blocks, and squeeze toys. Squeeze toys are especially useful for developing hand and finger muscles.

▲ Tape a pegboard against a vertical support or against the wall instead of using it on a table surface. Working in this position not only strengthens the arm and shoulder muscles, but also encourages mature patterns of hand movement for the later skill of handwriting.

▲ Make interlocking puzzles easier to complete by outlining each puzzle piece onto the base of the puzzle.

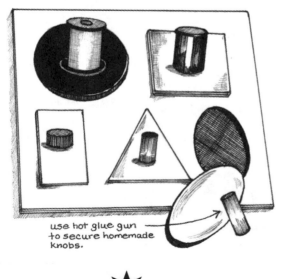

use hot glue gun to secure homemade knobs.

▲ Glue a knob handle to the top of each puzzle piece to make handling the pieces easier. Homemade knobs can be made from empty thread spools, soda bottle caps, empty film canisters, or short pieces of dowel that you can secure with a hot glue gun.

▲ Place manipulatives on the floor so that children can explore a variety of positions such as on elbows or all fours when playing. These positions provide lots of feedback to the joints and muscles of the shoulders and arms and help the child with low muscle tone and poor muscle development improve motor skills.

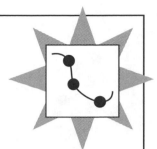

▲ Encourage children to talk about what they are doing while playing in the fine motor center. Use this opportunity to facilitate the development of language, social, and thinking skills.

Orthopedic Impairments

The child with orthopedic impairments needs to be positioned correctly to make the best use of his fine motor skills. The child's trunk should be supported so that he is symmetrical, not leaning to one side or the other, with the head and hands at midline. It is helpful to have the child's wheelchair tray or table at mid-chest level to prevent the trunk muscles from pulling down into flexion and becoming tighter. If the child's trunk is stretched out, it is easier for the child to functionally use his arms and hands. Some children with tight muscles may benefit from hand splints that position the thumb and fingers for functional use. Speak to an occupational therapist about hand splints. Children with orthopedic impairments should invest their energy in attaining those fine motor skills that will allow them to participate more independently in the classroom and at home.

▲ Self-help skills provide practice in many functional fine motor skills. The child should practice pulling zippers down, getting hat and coat off, hanging backpack up, washing hands, and other adaptive skills in the classroom.

timer

▲ The child's motor skills may be so limited that adaptive technology is needed for the child to interact with his environment. Switches can be attached to battery-operated toys so the child is able to activate the toy by pressing the switch.

Switch

▲ If the child has muscle tightness, avoid manipulatives that require a lot of effort to use such as stiff playdough. Resistance can cause tight muscles to become tighter.

battery-operated toy

▲ Instead of stringing small beads, the child can place larger beads onto a pipe cleaner. If the pipe cleaner is still too flimsy for the child to handle, use a thin dowel. The dowel can either be held by the child or inserted into a clay or Styrofoam base.

▲ Fine motor activities are difficult for the child with orthopedic impairments. Focus on the skills that will have functional uses for the child. It might be more important that the child learn to use his finger to press a switch than for him to learn to string beads.

▲ Match the size of the manipulative to the child's needs. For example, larger manipulatives are good for encouraging full hand grasping, while smaller

Fine Motor Center

manipulatives necessitate using fingers and thumb to pinch.

▲ Place knobs on puzzle pieces to make them easier to grasp and handle. See section on children with developmental delays for additional information.

▲ For toys that have activating buttons, enlarge them by gluing a larger Plexiglas or plastic button over the original one. Use hot glue or crazy glue to attach the Plexiglas or plastic button.

▲ To improve range of motion, encourage children to reach for items by placing the manipulatives in various locations on the table or tray. Include activities that allow the child to reach across his body midline.

▲ If the child has more tightness on one side (hemiplegia), turn the child's chair so that the more involved side is next to the table. The child will be encouraged to rotate toward the table and bear weight on the more affected side. This position may also help keep the child's arm on the table, thus helping to stretch out the child's trunk on the affected side.

▲ If a child has very low muscle tone, working with manipulatives on a vertical plane can strengthen the shoulders. For example, lean a puzzle against a tabletop easel.

▲ Utilize adaptive equipment to make fine motor tasks easier for the child. Use shower curtain rings or commercially available zipper rings to provide a larger zipper pull for the child to grasp. Provide Velcro closures for button-down clothes and sneakers. Pulling Velcro apart is a wonderful hand-strengthening activity.

▲ Glue magnets onto small toys and blocks, then use them on cookie sheets.

▲ Encourage the physical therapist and occupational therapist to work with the child in the classroom some of the time. The child may have much more voluntary movement after working with the therapist and be more able to participate successfully in classroom fine motor activities.

▲ Replace typical one-inch (three-centimeter) wooden cubes with cans of tuna or catfood for stacking. The size and weight of the cans make a stacking activity easier for children with movement impairment.

Pervasive Development Disorder (PDD) and Autism

Children with PDD are most comfortable learning new skills when they can practice skills frequently. Often children with autism need to practice fine motor skills on a one-to-one basis with an adult, because they have difficulty focusing within the group setting. The rate of learning is increased if it is reinforced by play time with a favorite toy, praise from the teacher, or a preferred food. Unlike the typically developing child, this child needs this level of guidance and structure to extract meaning from the world around him and to help him practice skills that he needs in order to achieve mastery.

Although the child with PDD or autism needs a teacher-directed approach to learn specific fine motor skills, it is still important to use the fine motor center as an opportunity for the child to develop social skills. Encourage all the children to share materials and work cooperatively with one another. Coordinate with the child's parents, therapists, and other staff so everyone uses the same verbal cues, gestures, and pictures to encourage interaction.

▲ Keep track of how successful a child has been at a task to determine when to move on to the next skill.

▲ Plan to include some hand-strengthening tasks such as opening clothespins.

▲ Work each day on self-help skills such as using fasteners in fine motor practice sessions.

▲ Adapt tasks to allow the child to be more successful. For example, when stringing beads, offer only the largest beads with a stiff wire such as a coat hanger, making sure to cover the ends with tape to reduce the risk of injury.

▲ Give this child only four or five of the largest nesting cups. As the child gets better at the task, more nesting cups can be added. Another way to modify this activity is to present only every other cup in the sequence in order to exaggerate the difference in sizes (Allen and Schwartz 1992).

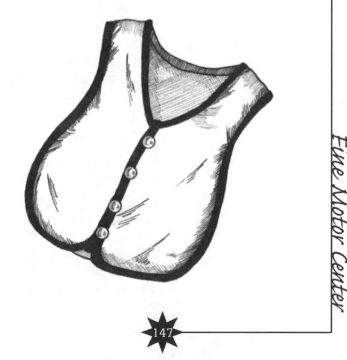

▲ Fasteners such as buttons and snaps are a great fine motor activity. When instructing these skills, break the task down into steps and teach the steps sequentially. When buttoning or snapping, the child must use both hands together. It is better to use buttoning or snapping vests rather than button boards. Some children have difficulty generalizing the skill of buttoning on a board to buttoning on their own clothing.

Fine Motor Center

▲ Many children with pervasive developmental disorders have difficulty tolerating tactile experiences such as handling clay or playdough. Let the child take small steps toward touching sticky materials. The child may initially only be comfortable picking up small pieces of clay and putting them in a container.

▲ Puzzles should have only a few pieces. When working on puzzles, start with four to eight piece formboards and progress to insert puzzles. Puzzles should have a theme that is of interest to the child, such as animals or trains. As the child is putting the pieces in the puzzles, encourage the child to name the objects pictured on the puzzle piece.

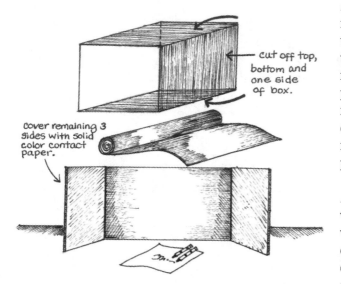

Cut off top, bottom and one side of box.

Cover remaining 3 sides with solid color contact paper.

▲ Once the child has mastered insert puzzles, move on to interlocking puzzles having eight to ten pieces. Tape some of the pieces down so the child just needs to figure out a few pieces initially. If the child has difficulty putting the puzzle together independently, use a black marker to outline the shape of the puzzle pieces on the cardboard backing. You could also put most of the puzzle together and have the child put the last two or three pieces into the puzzle.

▲ The child may benefit from a quiet place when learning new fine motor skills. It can be very easy for the child with PDD to be distracted. You can make an "office" for a child with a cardboard box. Cut out the top and bottom and one side. Cover with non-distracting contact paper and place on the tabletop.

▲ When teaching fine motor skills, sit across from the child so that you can see if the child is visually focusing on the task. If you need to sit behind the child, you may want to position a mirror in front of him to monitor visual attention.

▲ Don't expect children to fill an entire pegboard with pegs. Think about what you want the child to accomplish with the pegboard or any other fine motor activity and set reasonable goals.

Attention Deficit/Hyperactivity Disorder (ADHD) and Behavioral Issues

A child with poor ability to stay on task, impulsivity, and low frustration tolerance is at risk for unsuccessful performance in a fine motor center that is loaded with a vast array of manipulatives. With lots of manipulatives on the table, this area can be visually over-stimulating and may make the child feel disorganized and agitated. Some of the suggestions listed below will help you create an environment that helps these children stay on task and feel organized by using seating arrangements, dividers, study carrels, and containers. Developing a program that accommodates both teaching approaches to serve the different needs of all the children in your classroom will be challenging, but not impossible. We hope that the following modifications will help you in that effort.

▲ Place the entire fine motor activity on a cookie sheet or other shallow container to help focus the child's attention on the activity. Defining the child's play area this way provides some external spatial structure for the child who has difficulty with inner controls.

▲ Some children who are impulsive find that fine motor tasks requiring precision are frustrating. You might want to offer these children more freeform fine motor activities such as pushing golf tees or pegs into playdough, dropping small items into containers through holes or slits, or building with Bristle Blocks.

▲ Fine motor activities need to be at the child's ability level so that he can be successful. Puzzles are a good example of an activity that can be matched to the particular level of the child. Let the child choose a puzzle, but limit the choice to two or three puzzles that you have already determined are appropriate.

▲ Allow the active child to either stand at the fine motor table or kneel on a chair. These positions are sometimes easier to maintain than sitting in a chair. If the child prefers to sit, however, make sure that the chair is the appropriate height, with the child's feet resting flat on the floor.

▲ Another seating option is for the child to straddle a child-size chair that has been turned backwards. This position gives the child a broader and more stable base of support, which might make it easier for the child to stay seated for a longer time.

▲ Sitting, kneeling, and standing are not the only positions that might be helpful for the ADHD child. Lying on the floor while working on a fine motor activity is another option. In this position the child's body is pushing against the hard surface of the floor, which provides the type of deep pressure touch that can be calming to the active or agitated child. See page 183 in the appendix for a more detailed discussion on pressure touch.

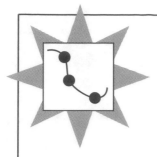

▲ Provide the child with choices to reduce the incidence of non-compliant behavior. Offer choices that are acceptable to you, but which give the child the sense that he is in control. Examples of choices include, "Do you want to use the Legos or the Bristle Blocks?" or "Do you want to put the pegs into the blue bucket or the red can?"

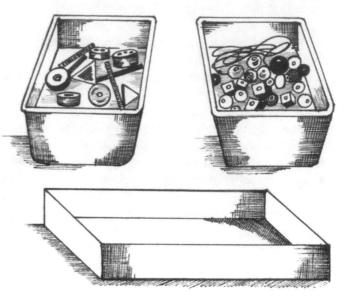

▲ Do not place too many manipulative materials out on the table at once. Choose one or two fine motor activities for the center. Place the materials in separate containers and use placemats or shirt boxes to help define each child's work space.

▲ Position the fine motor table against a wall that has been cleared of extraneous clutter so that the child can work with minimal distractions.

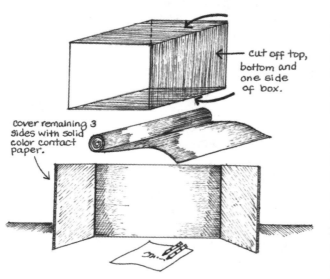

cut off top, bottom and one side of box.

Cover remaining 3 sides with solid color contact paper.

▲ Consider making a tabletop "office" from a cardboard box to help create a more private space. Cut off the top, bottom, and one side of the box. Cover the remaining three sides with a solid color contact paper and place on the art table.

▲ Provide the child with frequent positive feedback about how well he is playing. Frequently the inappropriate behaviors of a child attract more attention than the appropriate behaviors. When the child is not misbehaving, tell him so. Describe his "good" behavior in concrete terms, such as "You are really playing quietly with the blocks" or "You're doing a good job telling Brandon what you want."

Motor Planning Problems

Fine motor skills can be very difficult for the child with motor planning problems because the child has difficulty organizing movement strategies to complete tasks. It is important that children continue to work on overall strengthening and coordination while they are working on fine motor skills. A child may begin to avoid fine motor activities if he lacks confidence in his ability to complete these tasks. He may intentionally stay away from this center to avoid experiencing failure. Notice when the child is attempting fine motor tasks and give praise for whatever he is able to produce.

▲ Use blocks that snap together or attach magnets or Velcro to blocks to provide more resistance and help improve muscle tone. Resistance from this kind of "heavy work" can give the child a better sense of how his body is moving in relation to objects.

▲ Children with motor planning problems frequently do not use trial-and-error techniques to figure out how to assemble manipulatives and may try the same approach over and over, even if it is not working. Offer hand-over-hand assistance if you notice that the child is experiencing difficulty. Use cue words as the child is performing the task so that the child might later use those same cue words when attempting the activity again. For instance, during a bead stringing activity you can say, "One hand holds and the other pushes the string." The child might later recall these cue words to help him complete the bead stringing independently.

▲ Larger, heavier manipulatives may be easier to handle, although smaller items help to develop better finger dexterity. Start with items such as large pegs and rubber pegboards and after the child is successful with these items, introduce smaller, but similar, objects such as Lite-Brite. Use cans of tuna and cat-food for stacking.

▲ Make sure the child has daily opportunities to practice fine motor skills. As the child practices and gains skills, he feels confident, which will make him more interested in participating in fine motor activities. Once a child has mastered a particular task, encourage the child to try it with his eyes closed. What a thrill it is for a child with motor planning problems to know that his hands and fingers are so skilled that he can do the activity without even looking.

▲ Therapy putty is a wonderful material to have in every classroom. It can be purchased in catalogs (see page 190) and used to strengthen hands. It is more resistive and stretchier than clay and comes in a variety of strengths. Children also enjoy snipping putty with scissors or pulling and squishing it.

▲ Teach the child to talk himself through fine motor tasks and to employ problem-solving strategies. When the child is attempting a formboard, for example, he can associate a rectangular piece with a "door." The child can also trace the

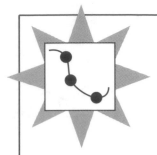

shape with his finger and trace the rectangular opening in the formboard to reinforce awareness of the shape.

▲ Some children with motor planning issues benefit from watching other people first. If you plan to demonstrate an activity, do not sit opposite the child. Sitting across from the child will present a mirror image of the activity and possibly confuse the child even more. Position yourself either next to or behind the child where your arms and hands are in the same orientation as the child's.

▲ Encourage parents to provide the child with fine motor manipulatives at home. Parents often report that their children with motor planning difficulties "don't like" fine motor activities and tend not to purchase these play materials.

Visual Impairments

Children who do not get sufficient visual information from the world around them frequently do not know how to explore their environment without the direct guidance and encouragement of a teacher, parent, or other adult. These children need more than a developmentally appropriate play setting. They need to actually be taught how to play. The types of interactions that you will have with the child who is visually impaired will be different than those with typically developing children. You will need to offer direct intervention in the form of both verbal and physical feedback. Talk the child through the activity, describe what he is doing, compare and contrast the objects and movements of the activity to other events in the child's life, and offer information about the immediate environment.

Although you should encourage children who have some vision to use whatever residual vision they have, remember that all children with visual deficits depend on their other senses to learn about their environment. The most important sense is hearing, but touch and smell are crucial too. Two additional modes of learning play an important role in the child's mastery of motor tasks. One of these "invisible senses" is the sense of balance and the other is the sense of where the body and limbs are in space. The latter sense is fundamental to learning how to work with manipulatives. Where do I position my thumb and pointer to pick up a small peg, how do I position one hand in relation to the other hand when stringing beads, how hard do I have to press in order for the blocks to stay together? Although children do not actually ask these questions, you need to provide the verbal feedback as if they did ask these questions by giving the child as much verbal information as possible about how he is using his body to perform the activity.

▲ Avoid hand-over-hand assistance and, instead, offer the child physical guidance by gently moving the child's wrist, elbow, or shoulder. This type of guidance allows the child to maintain control over his hands while exploring the object.

▲ Place manipulatives on cookie sheets or trays to define the child's boundaries. You can also use muffin tins to organize smaller items.

▲ Introduce shape recognition and sorting with just one shape, preferably the circle. You can block off all the holes except the circle if you are using a commercial shape sorter or make your own by cutting out a circular hole in the lid of a plastic container.

▲ Children with visual impairments might need to use their mouths to explore objects. Make sure that toys are safe and big enough so they can't be swallowed.

▲ Always try to have an assembled sample ready for the child to examine before he begins any manipulative activity. For instance, encourage the child to explore a string of pop beads that have already been assembled, as well as some individual beads. Give the child verbal feedback about the shape of the beads, the number of holes and bumps in each, as well as an explanation of why each bead has a hole.

▲ Use toys that make interesting noise or music. Sighted children are attracted to toys that are visually pleasing, and children without vision or with limited vision need to be attracted to toys by their other senses.

▲ Hold two assembled pop beads and encourage the child to pull one out while you hold onto the other bead. Provide the child with a verbal description of what he is doing. Allow the child to repeat this activity a number of times before attempting to pull the beads apart independently. Relate the concept of "pulling" to other familiar experiences such as pulling a wagon or pulling the door open.

▲ For stringing beads, tape the free end of a string to the table or chair seat to secure it. This intervention will help prevent the entire activity from being lost on the floor as the weight of the beads pulls the string down.

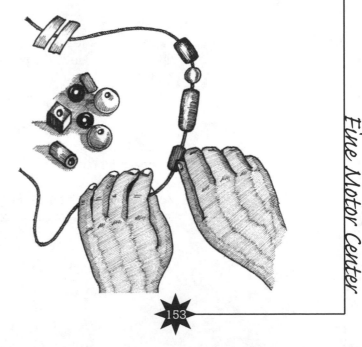

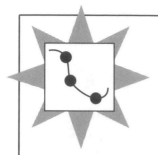

▲ Place manipulative pieces (beads, pegs, puzzles pieces, etc.) on a tray or in a shallow container so they don't roll off the table. Shallow containers include cookie sheets, shoebox covers, large jar lids, and tin pie plates.

▲ Use pipe cleaners instead of string to teach stringing beads. You can also dip string in glue and let it dry to create a stiff threading device similar to a pipe cleaner. A third way to create a firm threading device is to wrap masking tape around the last five or six inches (thirteen or fifteen centimeters) of the string or shoelace.

▲ Use metal or plastic washers instead of beads or choose beads that are squat instead of long so that the string comes through the other side of the hole without excessive manipulation.

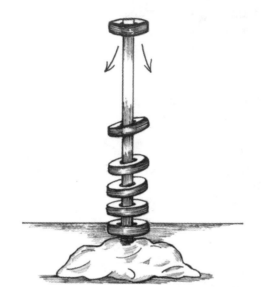

▲ Consider using a modified stringing activity such as sliding washers onto thin dowels that have been pushed into a clay or Styrofoam base for support.

▲ Choose brightly colored pegs or beads and use a contrasting color for the string or pegboard. Red, orange, and yellow are usually the most visible colors.

▲ Puzzles should be the simple, inset type with easy-to-distinguish pieces. Examples of simple puzzles include a formboard with a circle, square, and triangle or a fruit puzzle with a banana, apple, and bunch of grapes.

▲ Paint the inset board of puzzles with neon colors. For interlocking puzzles, outline each piece onto the inset board with thick black marker.

▲ Glue a knob handle to the top of each puzzle piece. The knob will not only make it easier to handle the pieces, but also give the child an immediate cue about which side of the puzzle piece faces out. Homemade knobs can be made from empty thread spools, soda bottle caps, or empty film canisters and attached with a hot glue gun.

▲ Sometimes you can find commercially available puzzles that play music when the correct puzzle piece is put in place. This type of toy offers wonderful feedback for success.

▲ Place a piece of non-skid material such as Dycem or rubberized shelving material underneath the puzzle base so that it does not slide around on the table.

▲ Some children with visual impairments do not enjoy handling unusual textures and might be averse to playing with clay or playdough. Allow the child to approach materials such as clay according to his own comfort level. Encourage the child to participate in the preparation of homemade playdough by adding some of the ingredients to the bowl or helping stir the dough.

▲ Another option for the child who is squeamish about touching playdough is to place some soft playdough into a plastic zip-closure bag. This way the child can manipulate the playdough without actually touching it.

▲ When activating a cause-and-effect toy such as a jack-in-the-box or a busy box, have the child place one hand on the part of the toy that will be "popping" while the other hand operates the switch, lever, handle, or button. Don't worry if you can't tell which hand is the dominant one.

▲ Choose assembly toys that do not require precise placement of pieces. Bristle Blocks are preferable to Preschool Legos or Lincoln Logs.

▲ To help the child understand the spatial concepts of block building, have the child place his elbow on the table while he stacks the blocks against his arm. Explain that the tower is taller at finger height than when it is only at wrist height. The experience of relating the activity to the child's body makes the abstract concept of height more meaningful. Use a similar approach when constructing a bridge; have the child build the bridge over his arm so that you can begin to teach the spatial concepts of over and under.

▲ Many children with visual impairments have underdeveloped hand and finger muscles because they have not done much independent exploration of their environment. Some of the modifications listed in the section on children with developmental delays might also be appropriate for children with visual impairments.

Gross Motor Center

10

Children are happiest when they are moving their arms and legs as they run, hop, jump, or throw. These gross motor activities are so important to a general level of fitness that they should be part of every day. For some children with special needs, however, these activities can be challenging. These children need encouragement to move. The strength, endurance, and coordination that children develop from gross motor/large muscle activities contribute to their progress in fine motor skills, play skills, and in the ability to engage in unfamiliar activities.

Gross motor skills in typically developing children often emerge in the following sequence. This is not a timetable, because each child's development is unique. Three-year-olds are not yet able to isolate movements of specific body parts and tend to move as a whole. They use their entire body when throwing a ball, and catch a ball with stiff, outstretched arms. Three-year-olds are starting to run more smoothly, balance on one foot momentarily, walk along a balance beam, or alternate feet when walking up stairs. They can jump off a low box and show some readiness to ride a tricycle. By four years, children have more independent movements of legs, arms, shoulders, and trunk. Walking and running are smoother and more coordinated. Four-year-olds begin to alternate feet when going downstairs. They gallop, isolate arm motion when throwing, and relax their arms when catching. Maneuvering a wagon is a skill performed by four-year-olds. Children who are five and older have more strength and endurance, improved balance and climbing. Five-year-olds skip, gallop, and jump. They move their bodies to catch an object. Five-year-olds use one hand to control a bouncing ball and demonstrate more coordination when kicking a ball (Gilroy 1986).

During gross movement experiences, it is important not to do too much for children with special needs. They need the opportunity to figure out how to get their bodies to do what they want them to do, to problem solve, and to make choices. Whenever possible, large muscle activities should take place outside where there is more space and children can move more freely, but motor activities can also take place inside as part of the curriculum.

General Suggestions

▲ Large muscle activities provide children with the sensory input they need to maintain an optimal level of arousal. Follow large muscle activities with quiet activities to help children to calm and focus on learning experiences.

▲ If the teacher is animated and energetic during large muscle activities, the child will be more motivated and focused.

▲ Gross motor activities can be integrated into the daily schedule as part of the curriculum, during transitions, or at clean-up time.

▲ Classrooms should have access to gross motor equipment such as tunnels, scooter boards, balance beams, beanbags, or koosh balls in order to include large muscle activities in the daily curriculum.

▲ Notice when the child who has motor difficulties attempts a motor task. Offer reinforcement when appropriate and encourage further skill.

▲ You may need to modify your expectations for how long a child can stick with a large muscle activity. If the child has muscle weakness or attention problems, she might lack the endurance to sustain activities. Children with special needs do not need to participate in gross motor activities in the same way or as long as typically developing children. Partial participation is a valid form of involvement for some children (Sheldon 1996). Build strength and endurance from the child's current level of skill.

▲ Encourage parents to send children to school in sneakers so that they can participate fully in gross motor activities.

▲ The child's current level of skill will provide clues as to which motor activities will offer the "just right" challenge.

Indoor Play

Space in the classroom for gross motor activities can be a problem. One solution is to store some of the classroom equipment in a nearby storage area or the hallway. Some schools have a common area, such as a gym, that can be used for large muscle play. Rebecca Isbell, in *The Complete Learning Center Book*, suggests making a fitness center in the classroom for the children. In the fitness center there could be an obstacle course and a variety of balls and other large muscle toys, so that children can be involved in active play. You can include gross motor activities throughout the day as a part of other centers or as transitions between centers. In *Integrated Curriculum and Developmentally Appropriate Practice*, authors C. Hart, D. Burts, and R. Charlesworth suggest that movement experiences should be integrated into the curriculum. For example, if the theme is "animals," the children could perform animal walks, pretend to be zoo keepers bringing food to the animals in wagons, or move to music about animals.

The following strategies can be used to integrate movement into the curriculum. Encourage children to use different walking patterns, fast and slow, giant steps and baby steps, walking on toes or walking on heels. Use certain kind of walks, such as baby steps to go backward or sideways. Include throwing and catching in activities. The child needs to develop control over her movements, not flinging or throwing herself around. Opportunities to learn to use the body expressively, sometimes gently and at other times powerfully, sometimes fast and

The Inclusive Classroom

sometimes slowly, contribute to the child's overall coordination. Encourage children to use heads, knees, elbows, and other parts of the body in large muscle activities, not just hands and feet (Hart, Burts, and Charlesworth 1997).

Movement experiences help children stay focused and able to use planning and problem-solving skills. Here are some additional suggestions for including large muscle activities in the curriculum that can be adapted to the needs of your classroom.

Children develop motor skills from the head down and from the center of the body to the fingers. Developing a strong trunk and shoulders is necessary before the child can develop fine motor skills. Scooter board play is wonderful for encouraging strong back and shoulder muscles. One way to include scooter boarding during the day would be to have children lie down on the board and scoot around to gather up objects to be used in play. A different way to strengthen shoulder muscles would be to encourage children to lay on their tummies and propped on their elbows while involved in activities.

Children should have an opportunity to play on their hands and knees to strengthen arms and back. This position also helps the child use both hands together in a coordinated fashion. Lay out a "road" with tape or chalk and have children drive small cars and trucks down the road while on hands and knees. If the road winds and curls it will not take up much space and the child can work on motor planning, strengthening arms and back, and having fun.

Encourage children to balance in standing, walking along a tape "trail" or balance beam from one center to the next. The child can also work on standing balance by practicing kicking a ball that has been tied to the ceiling or doorway with a string.

Obstacle courses help children to develop a sense of their bodies in relationship to objects and to become more aware of sensations from their muscles and joints, which can contribute to planning and coordinating movements. Obstacle courses also encourage the use of cognitive skills to problem solve and plan. For example, children love to play in a "car wash" obstacle course. This activity does not take up much space and can be easily stored after use. The children pretend to be the cars and crawl through a tunnel to be washed. The children can roll across a mat to "dry." Use a dry paint roller to pretend to paint the "cars." This is firm tactile input and may be easier for children with tactile defensiveness to tolerate. After being "painted," the child can walk on a balance beam or walk along a line taped to the floor to pretend to dry the paint and then go through the obstacle course again. Obstacle courses can be designed to fit many themes. A "letter carrier" obstacle course could be created for the community workers theme with mail being delivered along the obstacle course.

Children benefit from overall strengthening and motor planning activities such as animal walks, wheelbarrow walking, games that involve running in place, climbing activities, or fun seasonal activities such as pretending to ice skate on wax paper on a rug. While the child is engaged in large muscle activities,

observe if she is able to follow directions and focus her attention on the task. Be aware of the child's overall coordination and willingness to try unfamiliar activities. Can the child isolate body parts when imitating a movement or does her whole body become involved? These observations will help you to develop motor activities geared to meet the developmental needs of the children in your classroom.

Developmental Delays

Many of these children have low muscle tone and poor strength. Movement is difficult, so the child doesn't move, which results in more muscle weakness. It is important that the children be encouraged to have an active lifestyle in school and at home.

▲ Balance beams come in a variety of widths. Use the widest one you can find and lay the beam on the floor rather than on its supports if the child is reluctant to attempt balance beam activities.

place beam directly on floor.

▲ Some children with Down Syndrome have a problem with the cervical area of their necks and should not do somersaults.

▲ Place mats under climbing equipment to protect the child if a fall occurs.

▲ Exercise videos or tapes are motivating for the child. The video repeats the same movements and exercises, giving the child an opportunity to practice and enabling her to feel confident in her ability to keep up with the class.

▲ Encourage the child to persist in gross motor tasks for gradually longer periods of time.

▲ Always demonstrate the activity first to give the child some visual cueing.

▲ Movement and strengthening activities are especially important for these children, but children with low muscle tone may not be motivated to participate in gross motor activities because they are difficult. Make sure that the activities provide an appropriate amount of challenge and are fun. Allow children to watch a role model engage in the task before attempting it themselves.

▲ Parents should be encouraged to include their child in afterschool gross motor activities such as swimming or active outdoor play.

▲ Familiarize yourself with gross motor developmental sequences. If the child's gross motor skills are at the two- or three-year level, she may be reluctant or unable to participate in gross motor activities that have been designed for typically developing four-year-olds. The following activities will lead to success for beginners. Tell the child to pick up a beanbag and walk or run over to a box to put it in. Encourage the child to walk up and down stairs holding onto the railing. The child could jump off a low box, throw a beanbag into a container, or catch a large foam ball. Kicking a ball or beginning to ride on wheeled toys are other appropriate activities for children with developmental delays. Begin with one step directions in large muscle activities. The success that the child experiences in activities at her ability level will help her to confidently attempt activities at the next level of skill.

Orthopedic Impairments

Space problems are compounded if you have a child in the group who is orthopedically impaired. The child might bring lots of equipment to school, such as a prone stander, a chair of some sort, and a wheelchair. Some children might have walkers or crutches. This child will also need space to maneuver between furniture.

▲ Gross motor play cannot be a substitute for therapy, but you can work in cooperation with the therapist to have large muscle goals that would be functional for the child to be able to do in the classroom. For example, if the child is hemiplegic, with more tightness on one side, your goal might be for the child to be able to bear some weight on the affected side. You would then give the child some opportunities to play in side sitting, if necessary, helping the child to hold herself up with her affected side. Ask the physical or occupational therapist to show you how best to position children to encourage functional movements.

▲ Some children with motor and balancing problems may fall frequently during gross motor play and should wear a protective helmet and/or have an adult nearby.

▲ Observe if the child's involvement in a gross motor activity is accentuating abnormal patterns of movement. For example, if the child is struggling so much to propel herself on the scooter board that her muscles are tightening, you might offer the child a hula hoop to hang onto. You could pull the child or have another child pull her.

▲ During movement activities in the classroom, it is fine to assist the child, but slow movements are best. Quick movements might increase muscle tightness. Avoid always giving the child physical assistance to move, and encourage the child to do what she can to move independently.

▲ The child with orthopedic impairments who is walking may be able to do whatever the other children are doing, but for a shorter time or shorter distance.

▲ Occasionally, the child with physical disabilities can play the role of "time keeper" or "music director," by turning the music on and off during a game of musical chairs, but this should not be her only role. It is important that the child also be a part of the movement activity.

▲ You may want to consider some of the following movement experiences for children in wheelchairs (speak to the child's physical or occupational therapist to determine which of these activities might be appropriate for the child):

(1) scooter boards—children can work on head control and can either push themselves or be pulled by another child, with adult supervision; (2) therapy balls—children can reach for toys, with an adult demonstrating proper positioning; (3) ball pit—you can make a ball pit by placing small hollow plastic balls into a wading pool (balls for ball pits are offered in several catalogs listed in the appendix); (4) prone standers—children can practice throwing a ball at a target; (5) platform swings—give children a fishing pole with a Velcro hook at the end for catching fish made from textured fabric that will adhere to the Velcro; (6) wagons—the child can be pulled by another child in a wagon; (7) music—the child can imitate movements to music; (8) wheelchair mobility—the child can begin to steer wheelchair toward a target or around objects; and (9) balls or beanbags—children can practice throwing, catching, or hitting with a bat.

Pervasive Developmental Disorder (PDD) and Autism

Large muscle activities are usually a comfortable experience for children with PDD, although this may not be true of every child. Use large muscle activities as a relaxing transition after stressful times, such as riding to school on the bus.

▲ Use pictures to instruct the child about what she will be doing in large muscle activities. Many children with PDD are comfortable and coordinated in movement activities, especially those of their own choosing, but may have difficulty following directions in teacher-directed activities.

▲ Use motivating reinforcers for participation in activities.

▲ Start with one-step directions and gradually increase the complexity of tasks. For example, show the child a picture of a tunnel, have a role model demonstrate crawling through the tunnel, then encourage the child to crawl through the tunnel providing the appropriate reinforcement after a successful attempt. After the child has mastered one-step directions, show two pictures, such as tunnel and balance beam. Again the child could watch a role model, receive a verbal cue, "Tunnel, then balance beam," and follow the direction.

Show picture of tunnel.

Have a role model demonstrate.

After mastering one step directions, show two pictures.

▲ Gross motor activities can come before periods where the child will be expected to sit. Some teachers take their children to the gym to run each morning before entering the classroom. The children have been sitting on school buses and need an opportunity to move before they can be comfortable sitting again.

▲ Give children a choice of large muscle activities. Some children's nervous systems benefit from the proprioceptive input of jumping on a mini-trampoline, while other children prefer the vestibular input of swinging.

▲ Indoor motor experiences such as being twirled on a scooter board can be used as reinforcers for some children. Twirling should be used cautiously and is to be avoided if the child becomes overstimulated or has a seizure disorder. Some children can become nauseous from twirling or may experience drowsiness or headaches an hour or two later.

▲ Sometimes the noise and size of the gym is too overwhelming for children and they have an easier time with motor activities in the classroom.

▲ Having a rocking horse or other rocking equipment in the classroom can give the child opportunities for calming vestibular input.

▲ If the child is experiencing gravitational insecurity and becomes anxious when her feet are off the ground, allow her to bring a stuffed animal or other preferred object with her. Gradually introduce the movement experience, such as sitting on the tricycle with feet on the pedals.

▲ Involvement in motor experiences can stimulate language. Encourage children to verbalize and communicate to others during large muscle activities.

Attention Deficit/Hyperactivity Disorder (ADHD) and Behavioral Issues

Movement can be calming for children with hyperactivity and behavioral difficulties, but can on occasion be overstimulating and disorganizing. The large muscle activities need to be structured with clear rules and expectations. Observe if the child is becoming overstimulated and redirect her to an activity where she can calm and regroup.

▲ During active play with equipment and other children, conflicts can arise regarding the sharing of toys and following rules. Rules for behavior and consequences for infraction of rules must be clearly understood by all the children.

▲ Teach the children how to act in gross motor activities. Children need to be taught that there is no pushing, indoor voices should be used, and toys and equipment must be shared on occasion. Instruction in these skills will have to be given frequently until the child has mastered them and can remember them even in the excitement of play.

▲ Sometimes, children become overstimulated in large spaces such as the gym and are more comfortable with gross motor experiences in the classroom.

▲ Notice and give praise when the child is following the rules during indoor gross motor play (Rief 1993).

▲ Some children who have ADHD are highly sensitive to being touched and may perceive an innocent bump from another child as being a push. The teacher can explain to the ADHD child that no harm was meant, and to the child who did the bumping that the other child is bothered by touch. Make sure that the child has enough space in movement activities. Use hula hoops or rug squares to define the child's personal space during movement activities.

▲ Make sure the child is seated and you have eye contact when giving instructions.

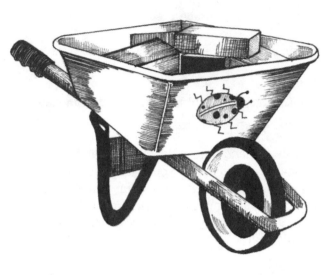

▲ Heavy work, such as moving large wooden blocks with a toy wheelbarrow, can be calming for some children.

▲ Attend to the children who are following directions, rather than to the child who is misbehaving.

▲ Wearing a weighted vest can be calming for some children. Refer to the appendix (page 186) for specific instructions on how to use a weighted vest.

▲ Structure gross motor activities to eliminate waiting.

▲ Keep activities short. A child may be able to stick with ball activities for a few moments and then need to move onto some other kind of activity.

▲ If you aren't offering a choice, give clear directions rather than posing a question. Don't say, "Do you want to walk on the balance beam?" if you mean, "Walk on the balance beam" (Cook, Tessier, and Klein 1992).

Motor Planning Problems

This child is typically aware of her difficulties in gross motor activities and may refuse to participate. Rather than expect the child to follow fast-paced movement sequences in a video or tape, use a piece of gross motor equipment, such as a scooter board, so the child can practice one kind of movement. Make sure to give abundant praise for any attempts, describing what the child has accomplished, "Good pushing the scooter board."

▲ The child may be experiencing difficulties with awareness of self in relation to other objects in space. I have heard an adult with motor planning problems say that she has to think about how to move through a door without bumping the sides, each and every time she passes through a doorway. Opportunities to move through obstacle courses will give the child practice in motor planning.

▲ Try having the child wear a weighted vest to see if that input helps to give her more awareness of her body in space. Refer to the appendix (page 186) for specific instructions on how to use a weighted vest.

▲ Some children with motor planning problems rush through large muscle activities. Running and other fast-paced movement does not challenge the child to use balance and controlled movement. Encourage the child to slow down.

▲ Give the child some one-to-one advance practice with a new gross motor activity that she is struggling with.

▲ Your participation in large muscle activities will help the children to stay on task.

▲ Any variation in the activity will challenge the child's motor planning ability. For example, the child who has mastered catching a koosh ball in the classroom might have difficulty catching a similarly sized ball in the gym. Variations of familiar activities help children to develop better motor planning skills, but understand if the child initially has some difficulty when the activity is altered (Bissel, Fisher, Owens, and Polcyn 1988).

▲ Positively describe all attempts at completing motor activities. "Good job trying to catch!" These children need lots of encouragement to combat the frustrations they feel with motor tasks.

▲ Children with motor planning difficulties should have active movement experiences at home as well as in school. Encourage parents to incorporate outdoor play as well as structured activities such as swimming or gymnastics.

Visual Impairments

Studies have shown that children with visual impairments tend to have poor levels of physical fitness (Warren 1994). These children will need lots of encouragement to move independently. Don't rearrange the furniture because that will make it more difficult for the child to find her way around the room. When giving directions to the visually impaired child be very clear and avoid vague words such as *this, that,* and *over there* (Mayfield, McCormick, and Cook 1996). Be careful not to encourage anxieties by being overprotective of the child with visual impairments.

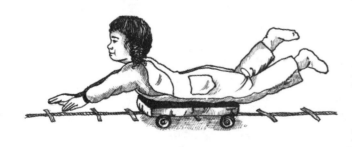

▲ Describe the movement experience or play equipment before involving the child. Let the child explore the equipment with her hands before attempting to use it.

▲ Tape a rope to the floor for the child to propel herself independently on a scooter board toward a goal.

▲ Teach body part awareness, laterality, and directionality. The child needs to be aware of how her body can move within or around environmental objects. Obstacle courses are a great opportunity for practicing this skill (Clark and Allen 1985).

▲ Use a gross motor routine or an aerobics tape designed for children, such as mousercise, to increase the child's independence in gross motor activities. The routine will help the child be able to anticipate what is coming next.

▲ When giving directions to the child with visual impairments, use the child's name to get her attention and give her additional time to process directions and respond (Cook, Tessier, and Klein 1992). Tell the child what will be happening next, especially before physically assisting her through a movement experience. Instead of just naming objects, describe them for the blind child (Mayfield, McCormick and Cook 1996).

▲ Surround targets for balls with brightly colored tape, or weave tape through child-sized basketball hoops.

▲ Direct more lighting toward targets.

Outdoor Play

Active large muscle play is best done outdoors. In fact, the NAEYC guidelines recommend that outdoor play take place every day. Watch the child to see if she approaches play equipment confidently or avoids swings and play equipment that challenge balance. Watch if the child is able to persist in a task or becomes easily fatigued. Note if the child interacts with other children when playing outside. Use these observations to plan outdoor activities for the child. Monighan-Nourot, Scales, Van Hoorn and Almy in their book, *Looking at Children's Play*, describe an interesting process their school went through in looking at their outdoor play yard. They observed children's play to determine where most self-directed play was occurring. They found that the environment encourages or discourages certain kinds of play; for example, sandbox play and digging encourage communication among children. The teachers involved in the study determined that they wanted to encourage social interaction as well as self-directed gross motor play and they structured their playground to encourage the kinds of play they wanted to see.

Outdoor equipment should include ladders, planks, jumping boards, and climbing frames. There should be walking boards of various widths placed at different heights. Rearranging the equipment is preferable. There should be a variety of balls from small Ping-Pong balls to large beach balls. Good visibility is important; the teacher should be able to see all the children in the playground to make sure they are safe.

The playground should be covered in a surface that will cushion children's falls. Inorganic loose material, such as sand, shredded tires, or pea gravel helps to

soften children's falls. This material needs to be eight to twelve inches (twenty to thirty centimeters) deep. There should be seventy-five square feet per child of outdoor space. Active as well as quiet areas, and sunny as well as shady areas, are needed. Before the children play each day, someone needs to check the area for hazards or vandalism. Trees should be pruned to seven feet (two meters) to avoid children getting hurt in branch collisions (Taylor and Morris 1996).

Dressing skills can be practiced when getting ready to go outside for play and when returning to the classroom. It is important that all children learn how to take their coats off and hang them on the hooks. Encourage the parents to send clothes that are appropriate for outdoor play, such as pants and sneakers. Remind parents to purchase jackets that are easy for children to put on independently. Nothing is harder for the child to get on than a coat that is too small and has a zipper that sticks.

Developmental Delays

Children with developmental disabilities will need some time to play at their current ability level before attempting more challenging physical activities. For example, the child may prefer to play in the sandbox, rather than to run around the playground or play on the equipment. Give the child a few weeks in a comfortable activity before gently encouraging attempts at unfamiliar tasks.

▲ Observe if the child is fearful of swings or other activities that offer movement or vestibular input. Although you should not push these activities on the child, you might try various swings. A swing that is low to the ground and has supportive sides might be more acceptable to the child.

▲ Encourage the child to develop her strength through climbing activities, always supervised by an adult nearby.

▲ Work on following directions in gross motor tasks.

▲ If the child seems to always gravitate to one piece of playground equipment, gently encourage attempts at new gross motor experiences on the playground.

▲ When teaching swinging, say "Feet out to sky" and "Feet under your seat" (Haldy and Haack 1995).

▲ Sometimes children are initially more comfortable swinging with their feet on the ground and their tummies on the seat of the swing.

▲ Play basic games such as hiding some toys on the playground and encouraging children to run and find them all.

▲ It is easier for children to learn to roller skate on a textured surface such as a smooth lawn area. When the child has learned to stay upright, she can proceed to skating on the pavement. Children should start with roller skates with wide wheels such as the Fisher Price roller skates.

▲ Use cut-up inner tubes as straps to keep child's feet on the pedals of tricycles.

▲ With an adult nearby, encourage the child to climb on large rocks (Haldy and Haack 1995).

▲ The child should practice running. If there is a small hill on the playground, have the child run up and down the hill (Haldy and Haack 1995). Try to have the child sustain running for gradually longer periods of time.

▲ There are lots of snow activities that make it worthwhile to bundle up and play outside during the winter: angels in the snow, snowman making, snowball throwing, spraying food color on snow, or being pulled on a sled are a few examples of fun experiences for snowy days.

▲ Incorporate community walks into the curriculum. Not only will the walking improve children's endurance, but it will help them absorb lots of information about their environment.

Orthopedic Impairment

Outdoor play may well be the hardest activity to adapt for children with orthopedic impairments. Adaptations will be expensive. Schools often conduct fundraisers to get adaptive equipment for outdoor use.

▲ Children in wheelchairs need some adapted playground equipment such as a wheelchair swing, or wheelchair accessible sand table that is on longer legs to allow wheelchairs to fit underneath.

▲ Observe the child's positioning on swings or in the sandbox to ensure they are not involved in abnormal movement patterns.

▲ Find one skill or activity to work on that will allow the child to play with other children. Perhaps it will be hitting a ball suspended from a tree limb or swing structure by a string. Make sure that the child's efforts result in a skill she can use functionally on the playground.

▲ A child in a wheelchair can work on improving range of motion while pretending to paint with water and a paintbrush.

▲ You can purchase a soft, cloth catcher's mitt and ball with Velcro strips. The ball sticks to the catcher's mitt making it easier to catch.

▲ Although it might be difficult for the child to go down a slide, she can independently roll toys down the slide to another child who can catch the toy and return it to her.

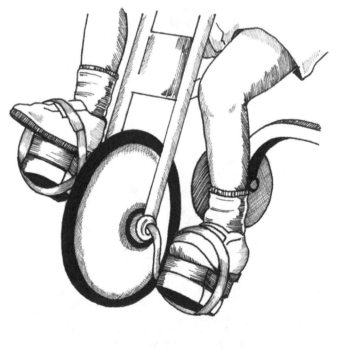

▲ Adaptations can be made to tricycles and other wheeled equipment. Build up the pedals with wood blocks. Secure the child's feet to the pedals with Velcro straps.

▲ Modifications of "Simon Says" that involve imitation of hand and arm movements can be fun for children with orthopedic impairments.

▲ Modify bowling games so that the child rolls the ball down a bowling ramp. This piece of equipment can be found in catalogs such as *Sportime Abilitations*. See page 190 in the appendix for more information.

▲ Throwing at a target is good for eye-hand coordination and range of motion. Adapt the target by making it larger and positioning it closer to the child.

Pervasive Developmental Disorder (PDD) and Autism

Typically, free play on gross motor equipment in the playground is a very enjoyable time for the child with PDD. Encourage the child to try a variety of movement experiences.

▲ Slowly push the child on a swing and pair the movements with a song to encourage language skills.

▲ If the child seems to be getting overstimulated, settle the child down on a blanket in a comfortable spot and firmly rub her back while speaking in a calm, soft voice.

▲ Teach skills for the sandbox that include interacting with other children.

▲ Incorporate sensory activities into the outdoor play experiences.

▲ Have the child take her shoes off to make footprints in the sandbox. Compare the size of the child's footprint with your own. Add water to sand to make drip castles (Granovetter and James 1989).

▲ Is the child trying a variety of playground equipment or is she sticking with one favorite such as the swing? Allow for plenty of time for the child to experience preferred activities, but gently encourage her to try a variety of movement experiences. The child may be fearful of some equipment, such as the slide. Break sliding into small steps, allowing the child to first just touch the slide, followed by going up a step or two and then coming down. Some children may be gravitationally insecure.

▲ For children with gravitational insecurity, playing on equipment that involves having their feet leave the ground is very frightening. These children will benefit from controlled movement input in a straight line, such as slowly swinging back and forth. It is best if the child can control the movement by dragging her feet on the ground to slow the swinging if it becomes too stimulating.

▲ Teach the peer models in the classroom to approach the child with PDD, take her hand, and include her in activities such as play in the sandbox.

Attention Deficit Hyperactivity Disorder/Behavioral Problems

Children with Attention Deficit Hyperactivity Disorder typically love to run and play outside. The concern is that with their levels of activity and implusivity they might be a danger to themselves or others if not given close supervision and firm guidelines.

Children with ADHD may need one-to-one supervision on the playground when they first enter the program. Phase out this support when the child seems to have learned the rules and developed some routines of constructive play.

▲ If you have the opportunity to buy playground equipment or make changes to your playground, avoid tall slides or other high climbing equipment.

▲ The child may benefit from calming activities when she first enters the playground and before returning to the classroom. For example, have the child swing slowly back and forth when she first gets out on the playground and just before the outdoor session is over.

▲ Weighted vests can be calming for children and fit nicely under the child's jacket. Use a lighter weight in the vest pockets so the child does not become exhausted during active play.

▲ Bring a book outside or a child's favorite toy so she can sit and play quietly if she becomes overstimulated.

▲ Repeat playground rules often and notice when the child is following the rule so that you can praise the child.

▲ Actively instruct the children in simple games such as hide-and-seek or things to do in the sandbox. Children play more constructively when they know what to do with another child.

Motor Planning Problems

This is the child who may stick to one or two familiar activities and needs encouragement to try unfamiliar large muscle experiences in the playground. The child may also have planning and coordination problems with familiar activities. You may need to break down playground experiences into small steps. For example, if the child is uncomfortable with swinging, just sitting on the swing without moving might be a comfortable initial step.

▲ Experiment with a variety of types of balls and ball sizes. Some children may find it easier to catch a koosh ball, beanbag, or a larger textured ball.

▲ Have a small portable basketball hoop on the playground for target practice.

▲ Use hula hoops for jumping practice.

▲ Invite a peer role model (another child) to demonstrate the gross motor activity before the child with motor planning difficulties attempts the task.

▲ Draw trails on the pavement with sidewalk chalk for children to walk along or follow while riding bikes.

▲ Give the child easy to remember strategies such as "Ready, set, throw!" to help her to organize herself during large muscle activities.

▲ If the child is having difficulty with a motor activity, tell the physical or occupational therapist. The child can practice the skill with the therapist and then use it during playground time.

Visual Impairments

Any child is anxious when confronted with unfamiliar large muscle activities, but the child with visual impairments has much to fear as she moves through the playground for the first time. She will need an adult nearby to introduce the different pieces of equipment, explain what they are used for, and help her explore movement experiences at her own pace. Often, young children with visual impairments choose "safe" activities that do not involve movement or exploration. The child needs an adult to provide access to playground experiences, encourage the child to explore, and help the child to interpret the experiences positively (Davidson and Nesker Simmons 1992).

▲ Don't take the child's hand and lead her around the playground. Teach the child to hold onto your finger while walking beside you. When the child is older and taller she can hold onto your elbow. This sighted guide procedure helps the child to get a sense of independent walking (Kastein, Spaulding, and Scharf 1980).

▲ When teaching a child with visual impairments to roller skate, put one skate on the child so that she is able to experience skating movements with one foot while keeping her other foot on the ground (Kastein, Spaulding, and Scharf 1980).

▲ The child can use a rope strung from one point to another to guide her independent movements around the playground. Be careful the rope does not cut across the path of running children.

▲ Make sure the child is wearing sneakers on the playground.

Bibliography

Allen, E., and I. Schwartz. 1992. *The Exceptional Child, Inclusion in Early Childhood Education.* New York: Delmar Publishers.

Ard, L. and M. Pitts. 1990. *Room to Grow.* Austin: Texas Association for the Education of Young Children.

Bailey, D., and M. Woolery. 1984. *Teaching Infants and Preschoolers with Handicaps.* Columbus, OH: Merrill.

Baker, B., and A. Brightman. 1989. *Steps to Independence, A Skills Training Guide for Parents and Teacher of Children with Special Needs.* Baltimore. MD: Paul H. Brookes Publishing.

Beaty, J. 1996. *Skills for Preschool Teachers.* Englewood Cliffs, NJ: Merrill.

Bissel, J., J. Fisher, C. Owens, and P. Polcyn. 1988. *Sensory Motor Handbook.* Torrence, CA: Sensory Integration International Publishers.

Block, M. 1994. *Including Students with Disabilities in Regular Physical Education,* Baltimore, MD: Paul H. Brookes Publishing.

Bredekamp, S. 1987. *Developmentally Appropriate Practice in Early Childhood Programs Serving Children From Birth to Age 8.* Washington, DC: National Association for the Education of Young Children.

Bredekamp, S., and T. Rosegrant. 1992. *Reaching Potentials: Appropriate Curriculum and Assessment for Young Children.* Washington, DC: National Association for the Education of Young Children.

Bricker, D., and J. Woods Cripe. 1992. *An Activity-Based Approach to Early Intervention.* Baltimore, MD: Paul H. Brookes Publishing.

Brown, J. 1982. *Curriculum Planning for Young Children.* Washington, DC: National Association for the Education of Young Children.

Clark, P., and A. Allen. 1985. *Occupational Therapy for Children.* St. Louis, MO: C.V. Mosby Company.

Church, E., and K. Miller. 1990. *Learning Through Play: Blocks.* New York: Scholastic Inc.

Cohen, L. 1992. *Children with Exceptional Needs in Regular Classrooms.* Washington DC: National Education Association.

Cook, Ruth E., Annette Tessier, and Diane M. Klein. 1992. *Adapting Early Childhood Curricula for Children with Special Needs*, 3rd ed. New York: Merrill.

Davidson, I., and J. Nesker Simmons. 1992. *The Early Development of Blind Children.* Ontario, Canada: The Ontario Institute for Studies in Education.

Deiner, P. 1993. *Resources for Teaching Children with Diverse Abilities.* Fort Worth, TX: Harcourt Brace Jovanovich College Publishers.

Downing, J. 1996. *Including Children with Severe and Multiple Disabilities in Typical Classrooms.* Baltimore, MD: Brooks Publishing Co.

Dunn, W. 1991. *Pediatric Occupational Therapy.* Thorofare, NJ: SLACK, Inc.

Edgington, D. 1976. *The Physically Handicapped Child In Your Classroom.* Springfield, IL: Charles C. Thomas Publisher.

Evans Morris, S., and M. Dunn Klein. 1987. *Pre-feeding Skills.* Tucson, AZ: Therapy Skill Builders.

Feldman, Jean. 1995. *Transition Time: Let's Do Something Different.* Beltsville, MD: Gryphon House.

Fink, D. State of New Jersey, Department of Human Services. 1991. *More Alike Than Different: Caring for Children with Special Needs in Child Care Centers.* Trenton, NJ: Educational Information and Resource Center for the Office of Child Care Development.

Fisher, A., E. Murray, and A. Bundy. 1991. *Sensory Integration: Theory and Practice.* Philadelphia: F.A. Davis.

Forman, George E., and David S. Kuschner. 1983. *Piaget for Teaching Children.* Washington, DC: National Association for the Education of Young Children.

Gaumer, Nancy, and Vicki L. Stoecklin. 1992. *Day Care for All Children, Integrating Children with Special Needs into Community Child Care Settings.* Champaign, IL: Developmental Services Center, Department of Children and Family Services, State of Illinois.

Geralis, E. 1991. *Children with Cerebral Palsy.* Bethesda, MD: Woodbine House.

Gillingham, G. 1995. *Autism: Handle With Care.* Arlington, TX: Future Education, Inc.

Gilroy, P. 1986. *Kids in Action.* Tucson, AZ: Communication Skill Builders.

The Inclusive Classroom

Grace, J. *Preschool Games: Terrific Transitional Activities for Your Preschool Classroom.* 1997. Westminster, CA: Teacher Created Materials, Inc.

Granovetter, R., and J. James. 1989. *Sift and Shout.* Lewisville, NC: Kaplan Press.

Haldy, M., and L. Haack. 1995. *Making It Easy.* Tucson, AZ: Therapy Skill Builders.

Harris, S., and J. Handleman. 1994. *Preschool Programs for Children with Autism.* Austin, TX: PRO-ED.

Harrison, F. and M. Crow. 1993. *Living and Learning with Blind Children.* Toronto: University of Toronto Press.

Hart, C., D. Burts, and R. Charlesworth. 1997. *Integrated Curriculum and Developmentally Appropriate Practice.* Albany: State University of New York Press.

Heidemann, S., and D. Hewitt. 1992. *Pathways to Play.* St. Paul, MN: Red Leaf Press.

Hendrick, J. 1996. *The Whole Child.* Scarborough, Ontario: Prentice Hall Canada.

Hereford, N., and J. Schall. 1991. *Learning Through Play.* New York: Scholastic, Early Childhood Division.

Howard, W., and M. Orlansky. 1992. *Exceptional Children.* New York: Macmillan.

Holbrook, M. 1996. *Children with Visual Impairments.* Bethesda, MD: Woodbine House.

Hutt, J., S. Tyler, C. Hutt, and H. Christopherson. 1989. *Play, Exploration and Learning: a Natural History of the Pre-School.* London: Routledge Education Books.

Hyde, M. 1983. *Is This Kid Crazy.* Philadelphia: Westminster Press.

Isbell, R. 1995. *The Complete Learning Center Book.* Beltsville, MD: Gryphon House.

Jackman, H. 1997. *Early Education Curriculum.* Albany, NY: Delmar.

Johnson-Martin, N., S. Attermeier, and B. Hacker. 1990. *The Carolina Curriculum for Preschoolers with Special Needs.* Baltimore, MD: Paul H. Brooks Publishing.

Kastein, S., I. Spaulding, and B. Scharf. 1980. *Raising the Young Blind Child.* New York: Human Sciences Press.

Bibliography

Koegel, R., and L. Koegel. 1995. *Teaching Children with Autism.* Baltimore, MD: Paul H. Brookes Publishing.

Koplewicz, H. 1996. *It's Nobody's Fault.* New York: Times Books.

Kranowitz, C. 1998. *The Out-of-Sync Child: Recognizing and Coping with Sensory Integration Dysfunction.* New York: The Berkeley Publishing Group.

Lasher, M., I. Mattick, F. Perkins, C. Saaz von Hippel, and L. Hailey. 1980. *Mainstreaming Preschoolers: Children with Emotional Disturbance.* Washington, DC: U.S. Department of Health and Human Services.

Lindsay, Z. 1972. *Art and the Handicapped Child.* New York: Van Nostrand Rheinhold Co.

Mapes, M., J. Mapes, and M. Lian. 1988. *Education of Children with Disabilities from Birth to Three.* Springfield, IL: Charles C. Thomas Publisher.

Mayfield, P., K. McCormick, and M. Cook. 1996. Adaptations for Young Children with Visual Impairments in Regular Settings. *Early Childhood Education Journal* 23 (4): 231-33.

McCormick, L., M. Noonan, and R. Heck. 1997. Variables Affecting Engagement in Inclusive Preschool Programs. *Journal of Early Intervention* 21(2): 160-76.

Miller, K. 1996. *The Crisis Manual for Early Childhood Teachers.* Beltsville, MD: Gryphon House.

Miller, S. 1994. *Sand, Water, Clay and Wood.* New York: Scholastic, Inc.

Monighan-Nourot, P., B. Scales, J. Van Hoorn, and M. Almy. 1987. *Looking At Children's Play.* New York: Teachers College Press.

Neisworth, J, and S. Bagnato. 1987. *The Young Exceptional Child.* New York: Macmillan Publishing Co.

Noonan, M., and L. McCormick. 1993. *Early Intervention in Natural Environments.* Belmont, CA: Brooks/Cole Publishing Company.

Novick, B., and M. Arnold. 1991. *Why Is My Child Having Trouble at School.* New York: Villard Books.

Odom, S., and M. McLean. 1996. *Early Intervention/Early Childhood Special Education.* Austin, TX: PRO-ED.

Orelove, F., and D. Sobsey. 1996. *Educating Children with Multiple Disabilities.* Baltimore, MD: Paul H. Brookes Publishing.

Peterson, N. 1987. *Early Intervention for Handicapped and At Risk Children.* Denver, CO: Love Publishing Co.

Provenzo, E. and A. Brett. 1983. *The Complete Block Book.* Syracuse, NY: Syracuse University Press.

Rief, S. 1993. *How to Reach and Teach ADD/ADHD Children.* West Nyack, NY: The Center for Applied Research in Education.

Safford, P. 1989. *Integrated Teaching in Early Childhood.* White Plains, NY: Longman Press.

Saifer, S. 1990. *The Early Childhood Teacher's Manual: Practical Solutions to Practically Every Problem.* St. Paul, MN: Redleaf Press.

Schwartz, S., and J. Miller. 1996. *The New Language of Toys: Teaching Communication Skills to Children with Special Needs.* Bethesda, MD: Woodbine House.

Scott, E., J. Jan, and R. Freeman. 1985. *Can't Your Child See?* Austin, TX: Pro-Ed.

Sheldon, K. 1996. "Can I Play Too?" Adapting Common Classroom Activities for Young Children with Limited Motor Abilities. *Early Childhood Education Journal* 24(2): 115–120.

Slaby, R., W. Roedell, D. Arezzo, and K. Hendrix. 1995. *Early Violence Prevention.* Washington, DC: National Association for the Education of Young Children.

Smith, R. 1993. *Children with Mental Retardation.* Rockville, MD: Woodbine House.

Taylor, S., and V. Morris. 1996. Outdoor Play in Early Childhood Education Settings. *Early Childhood Education Journal* 23(3): 153–58.

Van Dyke, D.C., P. Mattheis, S. Eberly, and J. Williams. 1995. *Medical and Surgical Care for Children with Down Syndrome.* Bethesda, MD: Woodbine House.

Warren, D. 1994. *Blindness and Children.* Cambridge: Cambridge University Press.

Wortham, Sue C. 1996. *The Integrated Classroom.* Englewood Cliffs, NJ: Prentice-Hall.

Young, S. 1988. *Movement Is Fun.* CA: Sensory Integration International.

Bibliography

Appendix

The Sensory Needs of the Child

Five or Seven Senses?

Sight, smell, taste, touch, and hearing are the five senses that are taught in school. We know that the senses are important in learning about our world, determining our likes and dislikes, and protecting us from harmful situations. The sensory process starts when our eyes, ears, nose, tongue, or skin receive information from the environment. The information is then sent to the brain where it is processed and interpreted into a meaningful message of action.

In addition to the traditional five senses, there are two other senses that we use on a daily basis: the sense of movement and the sense of body position. The sense of movement is related to the structures of the inner ear, which detect changes in head position. It is the sense that lets you ride on a playground swing without falling off. This sense of movement is also referred to as the vestibular sense.

The sense of body position is based on the information you receive from your muscles and joints to let you know where your limbs are, how your fingers are positioned, and whether you are sitting up or lying down. The body position sense is automatic and allows you to hold a pencil in your hand to write, chew food, or pedal a bicycle without having to consciously think about every muscle movement. The sense of body position is also known as proprioception.

Sensory Dysfunction

For the sensory system to function, the sensory receptors need to be in good working order. Sometimes receptors are temporarily impaired, such as when a child has a cold with a stuffy nose and fluid in the ears. In this case you might expect that the child's sense of smell and hearing would be affected, but only for a short time until the cold clears up. Some children have more permanent types of sensory receptor dysfunction. The child with low vision, blindness, or a hearing impairment regularly experiences the world differently than the child who does not have these impairments. This child needs to learn and practice compensatory techniques to master her environment.

Impairment of the sensory receptors is not the only cause of sensory dysfunction. Sensory dysfunction also can occur during the organization and interpretation stages of the sensory process. The central nervous system (brain, spinal

Appendix

cord, and millions of neurons) is responsible for processing and interpreting the sensory information we receive and making this information meaningful to us. That is why a warm bath creates a different emotional response than a cold shower and why strong rhythmic music makes us want to dance while lullabies put us to sleep.

Sensory processing difficulties can also occur in the area of proprioception or sense of body position. Children who do not efficiently process proprioceptive information from the muscles and joints efficiently might not know how much force to exert when pouring from a pitcher or when holding a paper cup. They might end up crushing the cup or spilling the milk as they pour with too much force. These children also have difficulty manipulating utensils, doorknobs, writing tools, and typical toys such as blocks, puzzles, and pegs.

When vestibular processing, or sense of movement, is impaired we frequently observe children with difficulty mastering gross motor skills such as jumping or riding a bike that require coordination of both sides of the body. These children often prefer not to participate in movement activities and might feel insecure when placed on a swing or slide.

Sensory Diet

Most of us have a sensory system that responds in a relatively universal manner. For instance, a warm bath relaxes the muscles and makes us feel calm. Other sensory inputs that have a calming effect on the nervous system include soft music, gentle rocking or swaying, cuddling, and having a back rub. Certain types of vibration, such as riding in a car, can be calming too.

We use calming sensory input on a daily basis, even though we might not be consciously aware of it. Sinking into the soft cushions of a sofa provides firm pressure to your body. This type of sensory input is similar to the calming pressure touch of a firm hug or cuddle. Prioprioceptive input to the muscles, joints, and tendons can also have a positive effect on how you feel. Proprioceptive input can include a brisk walk or jog, washing the floor, or chewing on the end of the pen or piece of gum. The total balance of sensory input that we need and use every day is our "sensory diet."

Sometimes children need our help to create the "just right" sensory diet. Children with behavioral issues, ADHD, and PDD/autism are particularly in need of our help. These children should be evaluated by an occupational therapist with training in sensory processing disorders to determine specific intervention strategies. In addition to the specific strategies that the occupational therapist suggests, you might try to implement some of the sensory options listed below. These sensory activities provide calming input to children with attention and behavioral concerns and can be used in conjunction with behavioral and cognitive interventions. (Note: Children with PDD/autism might need a different approach than what is presented here. Please consult with trained professionals to determine each child's needs.)

Proprioceptive Input

● Find "heavy work" jobs for the child. These jobs include washing the table or blackboard, pushing a container of blocks across the floor, giving another child a ride in a cardboard box, carrying heavy toys or books, moving furniture, and clapping erasers.
● Play weight-bearing games such as bear walking, crab walking, or monkey bars.
● Let the child wear a backpack with books inside or a weighted vest. Instructions for making your own weighted vest are on page 186. Let the child wear the backpack or vest for only ten to fifteen minutes at a time.
● Encourage resistive activities such as digging in sand or dirt, molding stiff playdough or clay, playing tug of war, constructing with Bristle Blocks or Legos, pouring water, tearing paper, using popbeads, and opening film canisters.
● Give the child "chewy" foods such as bagels, beef jerky, or dried fruit. See page189 for suggestions on fanny pack mouthing materials.
● Give the child a thick liquid such as yogurt or a shake to sip through a straw.
● Let the child climb a jungle gym.

Deep Pressure Touch Input

● Let the child sit in a beanbag chair or on soft cushions.
● Wrap up the child in a blanket or sleeping bag.
● Let the child put on a couple of layers of clothing or wear Spandex clothing.
● Put a sock-style hat on the child.
● Make a human sandwich—have the child lie between two gym mats.
● Encourage the child to pet a dog or cat.
● Give the child a backrub.
● Allow the child to use a fidget toy such as a Koosh ball, stuffed animal, squeeze ball, or homemade squishy. See page 187 for directions on how to make your own fidget toy.
● Hold the child on your lap with a firm hug. Let the child hug a stuffed animal.

Vestibular Input

● Provide slow, rhythmic rocking or swinging. Use a rocking chair, rocking horse, glider, or swing.
● Let the child hang by her knees from a playground bar. Supervise closely.
● Let the child lie over a large ball on her tummy and gently roll forward and backward.

Working with Children Who Are Hypersensitive to Sensory Input

You may have come across the term tactile or sensory defensiveness. Tactile defensiveness describes children who are hypersensitive to touch. Sensory defensiveness describes children who are hypersensitive to other types of sensory input such as sound or movement. Defensiveness is a very particular type of sensory processing disorder that is frequently accompanied by aggressive or self-injurious behavior and should be diagnosed by an occupational therapist who has been trained to evaluate this type of disorder.

The Wilbarger Protocol was deveolped to treat sensory defensiveness This program involves using a surgical-type brush over certain areas of the body, followed by joint compression. The brushing and joint compression sequence is repeated every two hours during the initial treatment phase. The Wilbarger Protocol should only be administered by trained staff since it can cause adverse reactions if it is not done properly.

All of the calming techniques mentioned above can also be used with children who are hypersensitive to sensory input. In addition to the Wilbarger Protocol, these calming activities help provide the necessary sensory diet that these children need. A special precaution should be taken to avoid any form of light touch since this type of input can be extremely irritating, even to the point of being painful.

Quiet Place

Create a quiet place in the classroom with a small tent, beanbag chair, or large empty carton positioned in an out-of-the-way corner of the room. The quiet place can be defined with sheets or fabric hung from the ceiling. This space could include a rocking chair or rocking horse. Sleeping bags or blankets can be used to cover the child and help her to relax. The child could listen to soothing music with earphones or look at books. Use this quiet place when a child seems overstimulated or anxious.

Positioning Guidelines

Children With Orthopedic Impairments

When looking at positioning for a child with cerebral palsy or other kinds of physical disabilities, first check the child's hips and pelvis to make sure that they are all the way back in the chair with weight evenly distributed. The child's upper legs should be resting in a relaxed position on the seat of the chair. The trunk should be upright and symmetrical, not leaning to the side. The child's head should be at midline, with chin slightly tucked in. The shoulders should be relaxed, not up around the child's ears or hunched forward. A lap tray or table should support the arms and hands. The child's feet should also be supported. The child should not stay in one position for too long, but should come out of her chair to sit on the floor, to use a prone stander, or to lie on her tummy on a wedge.

Children With Developmental Delays

Some children with developmental delays have low tone that makes it difficult to maintain an upright sitting position in a chair or when sitting on the floor. The child may have an easier time sitting at a table when using a chair that has arms. Always make sure that the child's feet are supported. You can make a footrest by putting sand in a shoebox and covering the box with contact paper. Children may benefit from a corner seat or other low chair when sitting on the floor to support their trunk and help them to maintain an upright position.

W sitting

This position should be avoided because it puts a strain on the child's knees and hips. In a W sitting position, the child sits with his or her rear end on the floor, knees far apart, and legs out to the side rather than folded in front. When a child sits like this, ask her to "fix" her legs and sit like a pretzel with legs crossed and folded in front of the body.

Augmentative Communication

Augmentative communication devices such as the Speak Easy, or Cheap Talk allow a non-verbal child to press a switch or button to access prerecorded messages that she can use to communicate with others. For example, the Speak Easy offers four minutes of recorded time that can be divided into twelve messages. The messages recorded might include essential communications such as, "Hi, my name is _____" or "I need to go to the bathroom."

Weighted Vest or Backpack

The total amount of weight in a vest or backpack should be monitored by an occupaional or physical therapist. If the vest has four pockets (two in front and two in back), then each pocket should hold only a quarter of the weight. Important: The child should only wear the weighted vest for interim periods of about fifteen to twenty minutes. If left on for longer intervals, the child will adapt to the weight and the calming effect will be diminished.

Weighted Vest

1. Use an art smock with pockets, a large shirt or lightweight jacket with the sleeves cut off, or a vest with pockets.
2. Add two more pockets to the back by cutting two rectangular pieces of scrap material (approximately 6" x 8" or 15 cm x 20 cm) and sewing them to the back of the vest along the sides and bottom. Place them at the same height as the front pockets.

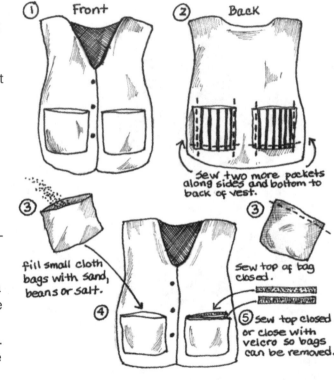

① Front ② Back

Sew two more pockets along sides and bottom to back of vest.

fill small cloth bags with sand, beans or salt.

Sew top of bag closed.

⑤ Sew top closed or close with velcro so bags can be removed.

3. Make the weights by filling small cloth bags with sand, salt, or beans. Sew closed. Each bag should weigh about / pound.
4. Place weights in pockets of vest.
5. Sew pockets closed or place Velcro strips along the top of each pocket so that you can remove or replace weights as necessary.

Weighted Backpack

Place books or other heavy objects into a backpack and place on the child.

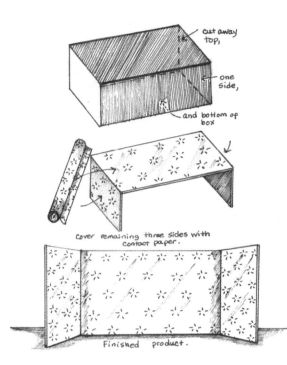

Cover remaining three sides with contact paper.

Finished product.

Tabletop Divider or Carrel

1. Get a large sturdy cardboard carton that is about 24" (60 cm) tall.

2. Cut out the top, bottom, and one of the sides. The three remaining sides will form a freestanding unit when placed on a tabletop.

Optional: Cover the carrel with contact paper. Use a relatively simple, uninteresting pattern or a solid color.

Squishy Fidget Toy

1. Pour flour, sand, or salt into a deflated helium quality balloon.
2. Tie the end of the balloon.
3. Take a second helium-quality balloon and snip the tip off the open end.
4. Pull the second balloon over the first to make a double layer of balloon.

Caution: Do not use this type of squishy with very young children or with children who might still mouth toys. Be prepared for leaks and breaks as young children love to pinch and pull at the balloons.

Another idea: Sew a small pocket out of sturdy material, leaving one edge open. Fill three-quarters full with flour, sand, salt, or beans, then sew up the last side.

① Sew a small pocket out of sturdy material, leaving one edge open.

② fill with flour, sand, salt or beans.

fill ¾ full.

③ sew up remaining side.

Appendix

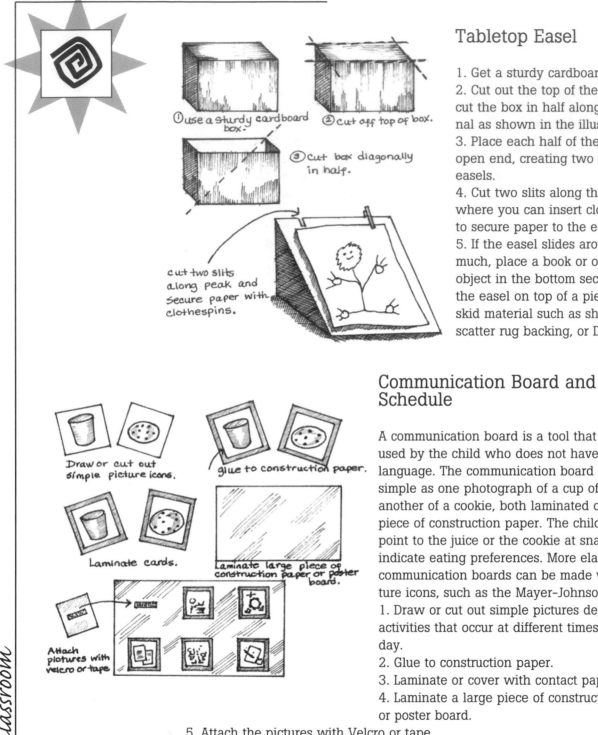

① use a sturdy cardboard box.

② cut off top of box.

③ cut box diagonally in half.

cut two slits along peak and secure paper with clothespins.

Draw or cut out simple picture icons.

glue to construction paper.

Laminate cards.

Laminate large piece of construction paper or poster board.

Attach pictures with velcro or tape

Tabletop Easel

1. Get a sturdy cardboard box.
2. Cut out the top of the box, then cut the box in half along a diagonal as shown in the illustration.
3. Place each half of the box on its open end, creating two tabletop easels.
4. Cut two slits along the peak where you can insert clothespins to secure paper to the easel.
5. If the easel slides around too much, place a book or other heavy object in the bottom section, or put the easel on top of a piece of non-skid material such as shelf lining, scatter rug backing, or Dycem.

Communication Board and Schedule

A communication board is a tool that can be used by the child who does not have verbal language. The communication board can be as simple as one photograph of a cup of juice and another of a cookie, both laminated onto a piece of construction paper. The child could point to the juice or the cookie at snack time to indicate eating preferences. More elaborate communication boards can be made with picture icons, such as the Mayer-Johnson symbols.

1. Draw or cut out simple pictures depicting activities that occur at different times of the day.
2. Glue to construction paper.
3. Laminate or cover with contact paper.
4. Laminate a large piece of construction paper or poster board.
5. Attach the pictures with Velcro or tape.
6. Pictures can be grouped and permanently laminated. For example, icons for ten toys could be laminated together on a piece of paper for use at play time.
7. Create a picture schedule with photographs of daily activities or icons representing those activities. Place these in the sequence of the day's events so the child can see what is scheduled first, second, and so on in their day.

The Mayer-Johnson computer program *Boardmaker* allows you to select and print icons for just about everything (Mayer-Johnson Co., PO Box 1579, Solana Beach, CA 92075, 619-550-0084).

Built-Up Tool Handles

There are a variety of ways to make writing and coloring utensils "fatter." Here are some suggestions:

1. Push the crayon, marker, or utensil through a 2" to 3" (5 cm to 8 cm) piece of dense cylindrical foam.
2. Poke a hole through a Ping-Pong ball using a sharp instrument or large nail. Insert the crayon, paintbrush, or other drawing utensil through the hole.
3. Wrap a heavy-duty elastic band around and around the grasping end of the writing utensil.
4. Some empty thread spools have holes that are just the right size for a crayon or pencil.
5. Tape three regular-size crayons together.
6. Break a jumbo-size crayon into 2" (5 cm) lengths. Insert one of these short crayon segments into a rubber tip used for furniture legs. If the tip is too wide for the crayon, stuff it with some tissue paper or cotton.
7. Use bingo markers instead of regular markers.
8. Explore your local hardware or electrical supply store for couplers, insulation, or other materials that might work to build up tool handles.

push utensil through 2-3" piece of dense cylindrical foam.

tape three same color crayons together.

rubber band to build up tool.

Fanny Pack

The purpose of the fanny pack is to have some items handy that children can use to calm or alert themselves. The following items might go in a fanny pack: mini-massager, surgical scrub brush, whistles, blow toys, squish balls, or pretzels. The child would decide which of these things would help her stay focused in the classroom. The very young child should only have things in the fanny pack that would be safe to use independently, such as a small sports bottle containing a lemony drink rather than candies that could be a choking hazard.

AbleNet *(switches, timers, adaptive technology, Speak Easy)*
1081 Tenth Avenue S.E.
Minneapolis, MN 55414-1312
(800) 322-0956

Flaghouse, Inc. *(gross and fine motor materials)*
150 North MacQuestern Parkway
Mount Vernon, NY 10550
(800) 221-5185

Fred Sammons, Inc. *(adaptive materials such as foam tubing, putty, adaptive scissors)*
P.O. Box 3697, Dept A 39
Grand Rapids, MI 49501-3697
(800) 323-5547

Mealtimes *(oral motor, feeding, and mealtime equipment)*
1124 Roberts Mountain Road
Faber, VA 22938
(804) 361-2285

Southpaw Enterprises (sensory integration and developmental products)
P.O.Box 1047
Dayton, OH 45401-1047
(800) 228-1698

Sportime Abilitations *(gross motor equipment)*
1 Sportime Way
Atlanta, GA 30340-1402
(800) 850-8602

Therapro *(adaptive, fine motor, and gross motor equipment)*
225 Arlington St.
Framingham, MA 01702-8723
(508) 875-2062

Index

Index

J

Jackets, 19, 46, 128–129, 130, 186
Jack-in-the-boxes, 26, 155
James, J., 79, 171
Jelly, 115, 126
Johnson-Martin, N., 14, 106
Juice packs, 119
Juice, 44, 123
   lemon, 58
   orange, 116
Jumping boards, 167

K

Kastein, S., 173
Ketchup, 53
Kitchen equipment, 26
Knives, 115
   plastic, 30
Knob handles, 144, 154, 188
Koosh balls, 31, 158, 166, 172, 183, 189

L

Labels, 64, 66
Lacing cards, 30, 35, 141
Ladders, 167
Lawn mowers, 31
Legos, 25, 29, 70, 94, 100, 141, 150, 155, 183
Lemon essence, 51
Lemon juice, 58
Lifesavers, 141
Lighting, 24, 57, 85
Lincoln Logs, 155
Liquid laundry starch, 62

M

Macaroni and cheese, 121
Magazine pictures, 61, 73
Magnetic tags, 22, 38
Magnets, 52, 146
Markers, 23, 25, 50, 51, 53, 57, 58, 63, 74, 75, 76, 148, 154, 189

Masking tape, 22, 42, 51, 65, 67, 76, 137, 142, 154
Masks, 61
Mats, 25, 31, 45, 54, 66, 94, 97, 100, 150, 159, 183
Mattresses, 18
Mayer-Johnson symbols, 188
Mayfield, P., 166, 167
McCormick, K., 15, 166, 167
McLean, M., 117, 120, 121
Mealtimes catalog, 190
Medications, 27, 107, 122, 125
Mental retardation. See Developmental delays
Menus, 26
Mesh screening, 23, 56, 57
Metal nuts, 57, 69, 70, 139
Milk, 120, 121
   cartons, 117
   shakes, 183
Miller, J., 78
Mirrors, 26, 27, 104, 125, 126
Modeling, 16, 24, 25, 56, 80, 105
Monighan-Nourot, P., 105, 113, 167
Morris, S. E., 117, 126, 168
Morris, V., 117
Motor planning problems
   art center, 56–57, 62–63, 67, 75
   block center, 98–99
   circle time, 43–44
   defined, 14
   dramatic play, 112
   fine motor center, 150–152
   form, 20
   gross motor center, 165–166, 172–173
   sand/water center, 84, 89
   transitions, 135–136
Muffin tins, 153
Murray, E., 20, 101, 103
Muscular dystrophy. See Orthopedic impairments
Music, 54, 162
   circle time, 33, 35, 44
   instrumental, 19
   soothing, 26, 27, 40, 182
   tapes, 31
Musical instruments, 22, 35, 38, 132
Mustard, 53

Index

String, 25, 29–30, 31, 61, 141, 142, 154, 159, 170
Strollers, 26, 104, 106
Stuffed animals, 22, 26, 34, 41, 46, 102, 183
Styrofoam, 142, 144, 145, 154, 189
Sugar, 52
Sweaters, 19
Swinging, 18, 54, 122, 182, 183
Swings, 31, 167, 168, 171, 172, 182, 183
   platform, 162
   wheelchair, 169
Swivel utensils, 27

T

Tablecloths, 19, 51, 77
Tables, 17, 185
Tabletop carrels, 16, 19, 23, 29, 141
   directions, 187
Tabletop easels , 17, 23, 52, 146
   directions, 188
Tabletop mirrors, 27
Tape recorders, 22
Tape, 23, 25, 30, 50, 52, 53, 59, 60, 64–68, 71, 72, 75, 147, 153, 154, 159
   Coban, 72
   colored, 51, 63, 68, 85, 97, 129, 167
   double-sided, 23, 60, 65, 68
   electrical, 65, 68, 71
   masking, 42, 51, 65, 67, 76, 137, 142, 154
   wrapping, 72
Taping, 64-68
   ADHD, 66–67
   Autism, 65–66
   behavioral issues, 66–67
   developmental delays, 64–65
   motor planning problems, 67
   orthopedic impairments, 65
   Pervasive Developmental Disorder, 65–66
   visual impairments, 68
Taylor, S., 168
Tearing, 69–70, 139, 183
Telephones, 26, 101, 106

Tents, 19, 26, 41, 111, 184
Tessier, 165, 167
Therapro catalog, 190
Theraputty, 50, 151, 190
Therapy balls, 162, 183
Thick-it, 122
Thread spools, 30, 50, 141, 144, 154, 189
Three-ring binders, 53
Tickets, 28, 110
Timers, 112, 125, 190
Tinkertoys, 29, 141
Toilet paper rolls, 30, 61, 141
Tongs, 24, 30, 78, 139, 141
Tool handles, 189
Toothbrushes, 27, 117, 124
Tops, 30, 141
Toys
   battery-operated, 26, 60, 107, 145
   construction, 26
   fidget, 24, 34, 35, 42, 183, 187
   wind-up, 30, 141
Trains, 82
Trampolines, 20, 41, 163
Transition cards, 28
Transitions, 127–138
   ADHD, 133–135
   Autism, 131–133
   behavioral issues, 133–135
   checklist, 28
   developmental delays, 127–129
   motor planning problems, 135–136
   orthopedic impairments, 129–131
   Pervasive Developmental Disorder, 131–133
   visual impairments, 136–138
Trays, 27, 154, 185
Tricycles, 31, 157, 163, 170
Trucks, 24, 25, 78, 84, 159
T-shirts, 18
Tubing, 24, 78
   aquarium, 83, 111, 123
   foam, 190
Tuna cans, 146, 151
Tunnels, 31, 158, 159, 162–163
Turn-taking, 42
Tweezers, 30, 141
Twisty snakes, 35, 42